FROM
CONVICTED
TO COP

FROM CONVICTED TO COP

PART II

SECOND CHANCES: STARTING OVER WHILE FACING SPIRITUAL WARFARE

(As experienced by)

TONY STEWART

XULON PRESS

Xulon Press
2301 Lucien Way #415
Maitland, FL 32751
407.339.4217
www.xulonpress.com

Paperback ISBN-13: 978-1-6628-3993-1
Hard Cover ISBN-13: 978-1-6628-3994-8
eBook ISBN-13: 978-1-6628-3995-5

Dedicated to: Colin Christopher Kittrell

Colin Christopher Kittrell, August 13, 2000–December 10, 2021
"Tetelestai"

Table of Contents

Preface

Yes, I was a convicted drug dealer. Yes, I was very violent. Yes, I have spent time in military prisons and city and county jails, and I later became a police officer with no criminal history. Impossible? Not when the master of creation walks with you. Yes, rage once ruled my decisions, and I gave up early on ever having hope for a peaceful or productive life. Today, peace has replaced anger, and I am no longer hopeless.

It would be easy to claim that my life's abundance of seemingly impossible events makes me unique. It does not. Similar events have happened to us all. I reached the bottom more than once, and like others judged hopeless, I gave up. What makes me different? How was I able to trade rage for peace and hope for hopelessness? While habituating in the bottomless pits of misery, I did pray rescue prayers to the creator of the universe, God himself. Maybe the difference was I not only asked for my rescue; I also asked to be a resource to my brother and sisters, who, like me, had given up on ever having hope for a future. I clumsily stumbled through my prayers with few expectations.

My words of desperation made it to the almighty God at a time when I had not fully believed in him. But, he had always believed in me and sent incredible rescues my way. He knew I would follow through on my pledge to reach others for him one day. There also existed praying people that were calling my name to him. Their prayers of intercession were an essential factor in my many lifestyle interventions. People came with their counsel, and some came to my rescue. He also sent his hoard of heavenly angels to intercede for me. And, yes, Angels can and do intercede for us in response to intercessory prayers.

In my first book, I told true stories of impossible rescues. Unseen angels delivered some from heaven. Other rescues came through the wisdom of people I encountered at the crossroads I traveled. I often slapped away helping hands and more often ignored good leadership. In my first book, readers learned to spot similar sneak attacks planned against them before damage was done. In this book, those lessons continue. But, this time, I know from where the rescues come. This time, new battlefields exist. This time the enemy throws an enormous army against me. This time I often see the attacks in real-time. Today, I can spot life's trouble traps more easily. The enemies' stealthy attacks do not always stay hidden. You, too, can learn to avoid loss and improve your ability to spot healthy life coaches sent to guide you. You might also notice a visit from an Angel or two.

I lived a lot of my life in the past, and let that blind me from seeing my future. Rescues were always nearby, but I let the evil clutter around me divert me into blindness. More specifically, I asked for wisdom. Yes, I asked for an incredible thing for someone like me. While on the bottom, I asked for the ability to see my way out. Slowly, healthy people, places, and things began to appear. They were already present, but I had overlooked them. This truth exists for all of us. We need only to pray for the ability to see our enemies and to embrace our earthly allies. And, maybe more importantly and often unknown is that heavenly angels also interact at the crossroads of our lives.

This true story will, at the very least, alert you that evil and good forces exist and are at work in our lives. You will learn just how well evil hides. You will also learn that good strives to show itself.

While my journey to hope started with only a tiny bit of newly granted wisdom, it evolved into the gift of discernment. This gift can be given to even the most defeated of souls. No matter how far we have fallen, we can reach a point where we can see life's trouble traps before we step into them. The road to hope took me longer than it should have. This fact does not have to be true for you or your loved one. I offer this incredible true story to illustrate that few have fallen further into the pits of hell than I did and returned. There is hope for the hopeless—always!

Getting Started

This story is true. As unlikely as it seems, It happened. I will list the actual names of the people who had a positive influence and not use the real name of some of the others. Evil is a living force, and so is his counterpart, Good. In the pages ahead, you will realize that more than ever before. Even if you already know each of their existences, you will learn more about their characters. One is your enemy, and one is your ally. Which one we embrace dictates the paths our lives follow. I Believe in making written lists, posting them in easy-to-see places, and keeping them current. It is also essential to create a map of sites. Begin to think about the roads you travel and the areas you visit as a battleground. Has evil already taken over the grounds you choose to walk?

Each of us can impact our future through the good or bad decisions we make. Seen and unseen influences affect our life course, but we can still change our destination no matter how many trouble traps previously snared us. There is always hope for the hopeless.

Why Do Bad Things Happen to Us?

At many of my life's past crossroads, death called my name, and unseen forces provided rescues. Sadly, I only realized this years later. I have previously written about some of these events but did not focus enough on the whys. During those battles, I was too distracted to see why so many horrible things came into my life. Instead, I only dealt with the pain of the moment. Looking back is not the best way to see ahead unless the story of my life can alert you to similar plans to slow or destroy you.

As I began to write, I also saw a fierce attack against my happiness. Death and Near Death was the name of those enemies. Some would give in to these forces. Instead, I am more determined to reveal the enemies that plan to rob us.

I can't write a story that will cure all your hurt. I can tell you from where the eternal healing originates. I can also alert you to life's trouble traps set in your future.

Why do bad things happen in the lives of so many of us? A significant effort is in place to distract us from seeing that answer. It is simply that evil fears our impact on the world. Yes, Evil lives. He is a supernatural being that walks among us, unseen or primarily unseen. Walk with me through the troubled crossroads of my own life, where I will point out how Evil worked against me from the shadows. On this journey, you will grow stronger by spotting his plans to slow or destroy you. Before we begin, let me add that it is easy to become complacent with our lives with far fewer blessings than God intended for us to have. Even if you already have hope, it can grow and become contagious. I did not become complacent.

Instead, I became defeated, and I surrendered too early. I lived through significant mistakes made by my parents and even worse mistakes I later made myself.

Real early in my life, I gave up. I felt there was no way my past could allow me to start over. That is a *lie*. Once we believe there is no hope for a happy future, defeat is assured. In my case, Evil knew that if he let me ever see a chance to recover from the mistakes in my life and start over, I could harm his plan to spread pain and loss. He uses the same strategy against all of us. You must realize that he cannot see our future. He can only guess as to our potential. Not being omniscient like our Lord God, he has to use diversions to sidetrack us from a blessing-filled future that he suspects we can have. To stop these truths from ever being shared, he used all resources available to stop me.

Don't Overlook Second Chances

L ife is a journey and has many twists and turns. There are road signs all along the journey that provide direction. Detours will always occur. Some are helpful, while others cause bothersome delays. Then there are accidents along the pathway that injure or kill. Missed traffic signals can cause accidents. Why do we miss traffic signals? Distractions are a common cause. The same pattern occurs in our life-changing decisions. When traffic is heavy, it is wise to stop in-car conversations, turn off the radio, and not use a telephone. Otherwise, an Evil named Clutter will join with his ally called Distraction and cause pain or death. Also, pay attention to road signs. They often warn of the danger ahead. Directional signs came also come in the form of advice from people. Some offer alternate routes that are healthy. Others intend to direct us to a dead end. Following signs on our life's journey can provide a second chance we did not realize.

Just when I started to write the introduction to this chapter, a song by Gordon Mote came on that spoke to me. The album's name was *All Things New*. The song playing was "God of New Beginnings." Coincidence? No. It was confirmation of what I should write. Long ago, I prayed and asked for such verification. It did not come immediately, but it does come, and it can come to all of us. This confirmation was not the only time music included a wave of our Lord's hand. Gordon Mote songs and other Christian songs have sent me the go-ahead before. Some signs are subliminal, and others are more pronounced. This one had a central message attached. This song's message is one of the second chances in our lives. This timing was not a coincidence. Instead, it confirmed that this would be the focus of this book. The evil one works overtime to keep us distracted. Signs are everywhere, but we miss them because of the clutter that evil sends to distract us. Evil also hates second chances. He does not have one coming.

I was not always a believer when second chances came. Still, Jesus Christ sent rescues my way. He offered me *second chances*. Even when I pushed His hand away, I had opportunities to start over. Chances even came when I was not yet his child. He continued to provide me with new beginnings. He cares for us all, not just for the Christian. He is loyal to welcome us at any time—mistakes or not.

What was His objective for giving me second chances? Why me? His plan included using my rescues to illustrate that there is always hope for the hopeless. My story will increase your awareness of similar events in your life or your loved ones' lives. Why did He send so many rescues to me? There are more answers to why than I can illustrate in a single book. At the heart of every recovery was a common theme–Love. He loves me. And he loves you. To begin recognizing similar second chances in your life, understand this.

Evil does a great job of hiding. He hides so well that many do not believe he exists at all. If you use this fact to explore the mistakes in your life, you may see him hiding nearby, coaching you into his traps. While we choose to turn toward mistakes, he sends his fallen angels to worsen our fall. Trust me on this. Examples are abundant in my life's story. By studying his battle plan against me, You can avoid future *trouble traps* and turn away from yesterday's false steps.

To illustrate these points, let me talk about rescues that came my way while I was still lost. Before I share those stories, let me say that even the happiest Christians are still under attack. We must not accept our gift of eternal life and retire. Someone in your life needs you. It may be a stranger, but someone needs what you have. Do not hide your treasure. Complacency is not the name of a Heavenly Angel.

Today I realize that I have often had a chance to start over. I usually did not see them and overlooked their origin. During the bulk of those days, I was a champion of evil. Still, the hand of the Lord was outstretched. Now that's grace. Even the most unlikely things or places can begin a fresh start.

In my hometown of Greer, South Carolina, a local restaurant was a hangout where my brothers and sisters from the drug culture loved to flock together. There is such a place in every city. Let's call this one the Back Row. I became a leader of that culture because I was more violent than most. I led in many ways, including distributing drugs to my back-row family. Often I would travel to the streets of Atlanta, Georgia, to make purchases and then return to the Back Row to peddle my evil. Before making each trip, I would take "pre-orders" and carry that money with me. This routine went well most of the time. On one trip, I ran into the brother of one of my friends in the Back Row. He had moved the 175 miles from Greer to Atlanta. He offered to help me make a large purchase. He took all the money, went inside a home to make the purchase, and snuck out the back door with my money.

On my return to the Back Row, I enlisted the help of a couple of tough men who, like me, were capable of being physically violent and intimidating. We returned to Atlanta fully armed. While we did not find that thief, we did find other drugs to purchase that we could sell to make back the lost money. Heroin was not yet a common drug on the Back Row, but we thought it could be. So, after buying a quantity, we decided to practice our hand at selling these new wares on the streets of Atlanta before we went back to our Back Row. Our thoughts were to get some practice dealing with this drug. There were all types of drugs to purchase. But the drug we chose was heroin. Until this time, using a needle to shoot drugs was not a common practice back in Greer. Such is the strategy of the evil one. He creeps his evil into our culture slowly. He planned introducing heroin to the Back Row through us—a word of caution. Evil is always looking for a doorway to come into our homes. Guard your doors, and watch the places where you hang out.

Our new heroin supplier had a nearby room where we set up shop to practice our skills. My first sale was to two men who shot the drugs while I watched. With their eyes swimming in their sockets, they complained that the heroin was no good and refused to pay. I was not the person to take being ripped off lightly. In addition, my two traveling friends were not, either. What came next was planned to end these heroin addicts' lives and put me in prison. I did not see it that way at the time; instead, I only lived in the moment, and at that moment, I was angry, and the evil named Anger sat on my shoulder and invited his brother, Murder, to join him.

I attacked the first man knocking him to the floor where he stayed. Momentarily, the second man briefly got the best of me but was also quickly on the floor. Why I pulled my gun was a mystery to me for a long time. I did not need it, and I had both where I wanted them. But I pulled it anyway. I remember thinking that I would kill them both. Who would know? My two companions from the Back Row were not in the room with me, and they had gotten away with worse themselves, anyway. As soon as I pulled the pistol from my pocket, one man tackled me around the legs. We fought, and I once again got the better of him. I put the gun to his head and pulled the trigger as we wrestled. The hammer closed on the skin of my other hand where my thumb met my index finger and did not fire. I dropped the gun, sliding it under the bed and out of reach. My back-row friends came in and continued beating on these men. With both of these heroin addicts beaten down, my friends robbed them of everything, including their car keys.

The heroin addicts were able to shove my thug friends aside and run into the alley. My brothers of misery chased and shot at them from just a few feet away. None of the shots hit their target. That in itself was a happy miracle that I only realized years later. We returned to the Back Row with no money, drugs, or bullets. Reasonable thinking people would say that our attempt to make back our stolen money by selling heroin was foolish. Just note that rational thinking is a rarity in the drug culture. For me, it was an instance of continued foolishness. Heroin did not make it to the Back Row through me. But it did eventually arrive. I was present a few years earlier when my mother overdosed on heroin. That lifestyle killed her when I was nine years old. I did not realize the danger of heroin after her death, and I did not see it after this experience in Atlanta. Evil hides well in plain sight. Heroin is also a living agent from Hell.

Second chances came to all of us that night on the streets of Atlanta. No one died, and none of us went to prison. None of us even thought about the need for a second chance. I wonder how those two heroin users' lives turned out? As for my back-row companions, one died a few years later in a gun battle with other violent men, and the other spent most of his life in a North Carolina Penitentiary.

This story is not yet over. Evil was not ready to give up. Months later, I was back in my hometown and stopped at a red light when I spotted the back-row brother who robbed me in Atlanta. As he went through the intersection, I followed him and checked to see if my pistol was loaded. It was. I intended to get even with him. I planned to follow him secretly until he got out of the car, then do a drive-by shooting that would end his life. Once the traffic light turned green, my plan for his death began. I was about three cars behind him when an oncoming tractor-trailer jack-knifed in front of me and nearly overturned onto my vehicle. He got away. Second chances came for him and me that day. He never knew how close he came to death. I did not realize that an Angel jack-knifed the tractor-trailer to give me a "start-over." I did not see this as a second chance until years later.

An unseen angel from heaven had interceded that night in Atlanta when I tried to kill the heroin addicts. I saw that as bad luck, not as a second chance. Years later, I played back the wrestling match with an empty revolver and tried to force the hammer to close on the meat of my other hand between my thumb and forefinger. No way could that have happened. I could not simulate it, but an angel could have and did facilitate that event. On the same train of thought, the tractor-trailer that jack-knifed in front of me was on a straight road, going no faster than 25 MPH, and there was no traffic in front of him. Was that also angelic intervention sent by the Lord Jesus? Yes. Overlooking such things is easy. But once you desire to spot the hand of our Lord, you can see it more often.

The heroin addicts and the back-row friend's brother in Atlanta missed death. During those events, I missed the visitor named Murder twice. For who was this intervention? All of us, that's who. I wonder if the others ever figured out that a second chance had arrived? I did, but I did so many years later. Over the years since, I have searched for other instances where things happened to push me out of harm's way. This search has heightened my awareness and changed my reliance on luck.

Is it possible that we can see an angel in real-time? Make a list of near-misses in your life. When I have asked others to do so, they always come back with a list. They see that an unseen force could have impacted the turns on the troubled roads their lives have traveled. I caution you not to look for proof. Instead, it would help if you used faith to open your eyes. With confidence, you will see more clearly.

Intervention is rarely just for one person. In this incident, several of us saw intercession. But, mercy also rippled through that time to impact my family today. I am also aware that intervention enabled the writing of this story. The same is true for the heroin user, the back-row friend's brother, and the thugs who traveled with me to Atlanta. Each rescue impacted future generations and not just us. We all saw intervention. What we did with that rescue was up to each of us. Why did intervention come at all? Why was it sent to such a sinful group as us? We are loved even in our darkest moments. Jesus is like that. He is love, sees our worth, and does not rush to label us hopeless. He sees our future and plans to forgive. His door to healing is always open. His plan included each of the others in this story and stood ready to send second chance interventions.

Each of these journeys had origins on a Back Row. As I traveled life's road, I chose Clutter as my constant companion and pushed peace aside. Still, second chances came, but it would be years before I realized this. Why did I miss so many directional signs? Indeed, they would have warned me away from danger. Clutter, that's why he is proficient in his goal to divert our attention away from God's plan for our lives.

As we sat in our Back Row, Peace often drove by and motioned for us to follow him. But Clutter had a more powerful hold on us. When the Back Row was my choice of places to spend my time, I led such a distracted life that I did not see that place and culture as a threat. Today on my map, I would draw a red circle around the Back Row and label it as a place to avoid. A few feet away from this place were also havens of peace and hope that I did not see or visited—yet. If I had created a list of bad events and an accompanying map of places, I might have missed a lot of traps set for me. I never kept such lists. That was a mistake.

Let me introduce you to my friends on the Back Row. While I resided in that place, I made friends. Do those friends measure up to my healthier friends in this story? No, but they were my friends then, and I cared about them. Back then, I did not think too far into the future. I never saw the day coming when the evils of drugs and alcohol would overcome my friends. I certainly did not expect Death to be a frequent visitor in my life. Evil distractors were common enemies to all of us. Those influences stayed so well hidden that we seldom noticed their presence. When you list such places and people, note that each area contains real people with burdens. They are all loved and are all missed. Don't write them off as hopeless. There is hope, even for the most troubled of people and places. You may be the doorway one of them needs to find that hope. In my story, many people combined to free me from the captivity of evil. Are you on the list of a person that has lost hope? If so, are you a healthy or hurtful influence?

Throughout this story, destruction and worse reached out. But, an unseen battle also raged to deliver me and others away from Evil's goal of destruction. Second chances, fresh starts? You decide. I made my decision. Start looking through the bad times. You, too, may spot outstretched hands of healing and hope.

Witchcraft Appears in my Crossroads

A fter my mother's death, my grandparents took me into their home. Grandmother Blanche Hall Stewart Lee and Grandfather Oscar Lee saw that I attended Victor United Methodist church. Even with that, I still gravitated to evil and was not a believer. However, at Victor Methodist, I did learn to respect Christians and the Lord Jesus Christ. I also met some healthy Life Coaches that would impact my life years later. The little respect I realized there would prove helpful later, as would these new friends. The following event tells of a time when simply claiming to know Jesus resulted in an unpredictable rescue, not just for me.

Victor United Methodist Church, 1 Wilson Avenue, Greer, SC, 29651, *Second chances began for me at this place.*

After suffering many terrible defeats, I did not give in to the tug on my heart until years later. But something in the character of that church and the people inside stuck with me. The words I heard there journeyed with me even during days when I chose to walk alongside evil. My time at Victor Methodist was short, but it gave me a greatly needed foundation.

After my Atlanta experience, I noticed a familiar young lady selling Mescaline in the Back Row. This hallucinogen was popular, so we met with my intention to buy a quantity through her. With the Atlanta drug deal still fresh in my mind, I agreed to her terms, and we went in my car to make the buy.

During our drive, she mentioned that she was a practicing witch. I untruthfully responded that I was a practicing Christian. My comeback was more of a way to debate her than a statement of any faith I had. Instead, I just wanted to bully and intimidate her, as all good thugs do, so I forcefully challenged her belief system. I represented myself as a Christian and claimed Victor United Methodist as my home church. They may have called me one of their children, but I had no right to use the name of that beautiful church in my conversation. Using the name of the Lord or his Church in the debate with this Witch was foolish.

We arrived at the home where the drug sale was to be, and she entered with my money to buy the drugs. She went in one door and out another with my money. My intent to bully her had failed. This girl was from my hometown, and I knew where to find her before she stole my money. On my return drive to the Back Row, I planned to get even with her. She could not hide. Would I kill her or just hurt her? I had not decided, but I had decided to do one of those things. Days later, I spotted her on the Back Row again. I reached into my dash to check for my revolver. Inside, I found all my money and her wallet with her cash. She had left it all behind. Who got a second chance, her or me? In those days, second chances rarely entered my mind. Instead, thoughts like these just got lost in the business of such events. Many Christians never encounter witchcraft at all. This instance was my first encounter but would not be my last.

Did she have a guardian angel? Did I? Oh yes, we both had Angels watching over us. She lost her money but was spared from death or injury at my hands when she left her wallet behind. Even the smallest of details often involve the unseen hands of Angels. Even though she claimed witchcraft as her belief system, she still had a guardian angel from heaven. And so do we all. Second chances are abundant and all around us. That day, neither she nor I thought about Angels. Is there a hidden force working to distract us from realizing that such intervention exists? Oh yes. This invisible force is constantly at work and is a champion of distraction. Advocates from heaven fought for both of us that day.

Second chances come so frequently that their number is impossible to count. This battle between Evil and Good often raged around the back-row culture. But we did not know that it existed. Second chances were thought of occasionally but only as a factor of good or bad luck. Sadly, the evil forces claimed victories over many of my brothers and sisters from the Back Row—some far too early in life. Hidden forces pushed us all into harm's way while we eagerly volunteered to travel those troubled roads.

Witchcraft has visited me several times. He would try to lure me into his trap. He would even invite me to join him. His failed attempts to recruit me eventually became an all-out assault to destroy me. He came out of the dark and into the open when I became a police officer in my hometown. Yes, I was once a bully, a violent thug, and a drug dealer. I was even caught selling drugs to an undercover agent and spent time in jail more than once. Since it takes a spotless criminal history to become a peace officer, how was this possible? My response is not how but why? It was so that I could write this story of how anyone can loosen the evil grip from their throats. More to follow about this is ahead. This story is not fiction. It is all true, and similar rescues can come to anyone. Second chances are always nearby, even for a drug dealer and a witch.

On a typical day on the Back Row, the hidden forces of Evil fought against the agents of Good for all of our welfare. Peace and clearness of thought were often wounded. Pain, Addiction, and Death celebrated their victories. These battles were for all of us and not just for Christians. Today, I see them walking among us on the Back Row as I look back. Oh, how I wished I could have alerted my Back Row friends.

The young lady who chose witchcraft was popular among us on the Back Row. It was easy to call her a friend. Like the rest of us, she made mistakes and gravitated to the Back Row, where she felt more comfort from us than in healthy places in her life. This feeling was shared among us who chose the Back Row instead of our homes. I disagreed with her choice of witchcraft, but she became my friend anyway. One day she was never seen again in the Back Row. I have often wondered if she ran out of second chances before turning to the Lord Jesus. I pray that she did not.

What Hidden Forces?

What hidden forces? First, let's rule out luck as the prime reason for unexpected turns in our lives. We have the gift of free will. We can use it to make our own decisions. Call the outcomes luck, if you will. But unseen influencers surround us that stand ready to help us toward or divert us away from our choice of destinations. Knowing this can impact your future more than waiting for your luck to change. My writing goal is to increase the awareness of unseen agents in our lives. They do exist. If you are not already a believer in the existence of Good and Evil, it may be because you have not met Evil as often as I did. Evil is the more pronounced of the two forces, and he often appears. He is coming out of hiding more often because our life choices invite him to no longer hide. If he has stayed wholly hidden in your life, consider that he may think he already owns you. Good, on the other hand, works to reveal himself whenever possible. It takes faith in Jesus Christ to see the hand of God working in our lives. Without faith, you will probably miss his influence at the crossroads of your lives. In my life, I saw the power of good only after I became a Christian. However, it was always nearby, ready with second chances.

Is there proof of hidden forces? Read on, and you will find things that no other logic can explain. If you read with an open mind, a belief solely in luck will lose its grip on your powers of reason. Remember that the most potent skill of Satan is to make us believe that he does not exist at all. On the other hand, the Lord Jesus strives to show himself as your savior at all times. Many of my rescues were factors of unseen battles fought for me. But there were times when I saw His hand in real-time. Even when I was lost, I spotted Evil occasionally. However, I ignored signs of healing and hope in my sin-filled life.

Let me share a time when Evil did not hide. Most of us on the Back Row took every opportunity to attend concerts, but instead of enjoying the music, I would work through the crowd, selling drugs. I would mainly sell things that could fit into my pockets: hallucinogens, speed, and barbiturates. Cocaine was also a product of mine but not at concerts. My concert routine was to keep my pockets full and enlist lovely lady friends from the Back Row to work the concert audience. I often made numerous trips to our car in the parking lot to refill my pockets. I bought many tickets to reenter most concerts. Occasionally I would team up with another man from the Back Row with a similar reputation as mine. Wayne, like I was physically skilled with his hands. He, too, was very good at being very bad. He passed away a few years back. But not before he turned his life to Christ. He became very proficient at being a witness for Jesus.

At one sweltering summer concert, Murder again visited and brought many of his allies with him. On this particular day, evil forces that usually stayed hidden came out into the open. The concert was an open-air version, where the band and the crowd were outside on the grass. Wayne and another man went into the group of listeners to peddle our wares. I chose a hill that overlooked the entire event as the place to operate. At these events, we decided not to get high. It was a business day for us, so what I tell you was not influenced by drugs or alcohol. A vendor was selling ice-cold slices of watermelons. I could see the entire crowd from my location and noticed one man walking around the edges picking up the leftover watermelon rinds and pitching them into the air and toward the groups of people. No one ever noticed where the melons came from that hit them. I observed him as he danced around madly, laughing and shouting. Evil was no longer hiding. He made an arrogant appearance, and few noticed him. This kind of bold appearance is more common than most know.

The crowd got unruly. The police came and fired tear gas into the crowd below me. The officers were too far back for the tear gas to reach the masses. This enraged dancer picked up each canister and threw them deeper into the crowd, just as he had done with the watermelons. Somehow, where each of the tear gas rounds fired by the officers landed, he was always right there. After the smoke cleared, I watched as he moved away from the crowd and disappeared. I sat on that hill for several more hours and never saw him again. Was he Evil that dared to show himself? At the time, I did not consider this a fact. Today, I think differently. Maybe he was evil personified. Perhaps he was dancing his victory dance because of the pain he would inflict.

Today, I know that Evil often dares to show itself. Satan is constantly at work to remove our sensitivity to his ways. Evidence is in the decay of family values. And more distinctly, the very definition of family values has changed because of his continued attacks. The influence of Evil can take years to develop before he decides to show himself. Satan can and does use all resources, including television, movies, and concerts.

That day was not yet over. As the day-long concert ended, my two drug-supplying partners and I headed to our parked car. We never let the ladies who peddled our drugs to the crowds travel with us, so it was just the three of us. Eight to ten men were standing in front of our car, drinking, and blocking our exit. We asked them to move away so that we could drive off. They refused and came to my window to argue with us. The three of us evacuated our car into this fired-up group of men. Wayne and I were both proficient with our hands, so we quickly got the upper hand and left several of that group lying on the ground. When I had won my battles, I noticed that Wayne was still battling with two men on the other side of the car. These were the only two left, as all the others had run away or were still on the ground. What happened next was not needed. Wayne was winning his fight and did not need my help. However, I reached into our dash and pulled out my revolver. In battles, I had learned always to be aware of my surroundings. I looked around to confirm that no one was anywhere near me. As I went toward Wayne, I intended to shoot both of his combatants. The evil agent of Murder had arrived again and was an unseen force pushing me forward.

Suddenly two tall men dressed all in white appeared on either side of me. They lifted me off my feet by my elbows and said in unison, " You don't want to do this." They carried me back to the front seat of our car, took my pistol, and were gone. The Angels of Second Chances had appeared. I was to receive another *Second Chance*. Or were they the rescuers of the other two men instead? We were fighting near the exit, and several carloads of back-row brothers and sisters passed us as we battled. Our victories planted seeds that day that gave both of us reputations as people to fear.

Evil appeared that day. Good also appeared. But the battles were not yet over. We had left beer in our car. It was hot, but we drank it on the road home to celebrate our victories. Wayne was driving and glanced off a bridge on our drive back to the Back Row. We bounced back safely onto the roadway. All around us were very steep drop-offs that ended in a deep lake. The only place to run off the road and not die was on that bridge. Hidden evil intended to kill us that day. We wrote these events off as luck. Bad luck or good luck was our ruling. We never considered outside influences at all. What do you think? Second chances are what I believe. Do you believe in them? They do come, but what we do with them is the real question.

The Back Row saw many deaths due to lifestyle choices. For each of them, I now wonder if they ever responded to the heavenly interventions sent their way before they died. Counting on the liar named Luck is a foolish way to navigate life. In too many cases, members of our back-row family died, and luck had nothing to do with it. This event at the concert was one of the first that made me curious about outside forces acting on my life. I began to make mental lists of other such events. This curiosity improved my awareness, and I started seeing more interactions than I had ever seen. While I can't use this to prove anything to those who don't yet have faith in Jesus Christ, I will say that you will improve your vision with such a study. I challenge you to take a few steps away from the clutter and watch the traffic of the people you will observe. Do this a few times, and you too will spot Evil hiding in plain sight.

Is Intercession Only for Christians?

The stories so far focus on just a few of the crossroads of my life where battles raged. But the wars fought over me started much earlier in my life. The same is true for all of us—good and evil forces battle for us daily. Intercession is not just for Christians. It came for me before I called Jesus my Lord. I thought the interventions I saw were for me alone for a long time. I was wrong. The stories I share include others who saw mercy, like the thief from Atlanta, the Witch, and the last two men at the concert that Wayne battled. This knowledge has made me reevaluate all of the rescues I saw. Now I more fully understand what mercy is. When I judged others as unworthy enemies of mine, the Lord saw them as His children. Intervention is not just for Christians. The Lord Jesus never tires of sending rescues to you or me. His death on the cross and subsequent resurrection were the ultimate intercession act.

My childhood saw things adults should not experience from ages seven to nine. Those horrible things lessened when my mother used heroin for the last time. It was tough to understand that her death was my rescue, and it would be years before I fully knew this. I have no names for the men of those days, just a memory of their deeds to her and me. I am left to wonder how they turned out? Did they ever realize that forgiveness and a fresh start was so close? Intercessions were made for me before I was a Christian. Did such intervention come to any of them? I pray that it did.

The back-row culture taught me that sudden death was a frequent occurrence. Our lifestyle choices fueled this outcome. I grieve that my back-row brothers and sisters who never claimed Jesus was–eternally lost. I realized that I was saved while living in my sin and prayed that this might have been true for them. Prayerfully, the same mediation might also have been true for those evil men in the memories of my younger years.

Coming out of those days of being surrounded by evil deeds, I saw sacred ground at my grandparents' home. I saw a healthy kind of love, and it gained a place in my heart. This move was my time to start over. At nine years of age, I got a fresh start. Today I know that second chances always point to new beginnings. I also know that we rarely realize this. Diversion, Deception, and Distraction are just a few evils sent to rob us of recognizing a chance to start over. Second chances evolve into fresh starts, which bothers the fallen angel Satan. He goes into high gear to stop us from under-standing that second chances often come right after a train wreck in our life's journey.

Before the death of my mother, I was not a Christian. Before living in my grandparents' home, I did not often hear the name of Jesus. Even at Christmas time, I have no memories of why we celebrated that holiday. The tragic death of my mother made my new home possible. This fresh start came before I was a Christian and knew this lifestyle existed. Intercession can come to a non-Christian.

Soon after this move, trips to church replaced trips to the rooms of strange men my mother chose. Worship and praise replaced acts that I will not describe here. I met healthy people. Hope was growing but becoming a Christian myself was not yet a reality. Still, second chances came. A strong word of advice here is you–cannot hold Jesus accountable for the times when you refuse His rescues.

Intercession was at work for me while and before I was a Christian. People had my name on their hearts, and this was not new. My future was in the hearts of these earthly warriors for a long time. Today, my intercessory prayers are for you, my reader. The back-row culture included a lot of people who were searching for a supportive family. Like many, I had relatives of a healthy character living nearby to fill that role. But, bad decisions created a distance between us and those who stood ready to embrace us. On the Back Row, we found unhealthy replacements. We also chose to use drugs and alcohol to drown out the unseen forces of Good. Good often whispers, while Evil shouts. And sadly, we most often choose to follow the loudest voice. Such is the role of a sheep. We follow any shepherd who loudly claims to be a leader. I offer this fact only after I learned it through the school of hard knocks. I lost many of my back-row family because they followed the wrong shepherd down a trail that led to their death. Where can you find good shepherds today? In the house of our Lord Jesus Christ, of course. The work of mediation stands ready to direct all of us to places and people of peace and hope. The Back Row culture fueled distractions. Accordingly, we all often missed rescue attempts and sound advice. Today, I choose to be more cautious with the guidance of strangers I meet. Rush and Haste were the joint forces that used me too often. The most damaging influences can change from person to person. For me, Haste often cluttered my thinking.

Like angels assigned to principalities, there are also influencing Angels assigned for every influence of Good; *Psalm 91:11*, or Evil; *Ephesians 6:12-18*. Naming them makes it easier for us to realize they exist. Names for the Agents of Evil include Demons and Devils; *James 2:19*.

Early Mistakes That Open Doors

To better understand my story, I will share my choices that invited mistakes into my life. Mistakes often lead to trouble, and the migration to more significant loss grows stronger with each door opened. The result is that we can't find our way back to a fresh start. Follow me as I journey back in time to illustrate how one doorway led to another, and I soon became lost inside my choices. Promoting these mistakes is a fundamental goal of the fallen angel Satan. If he can get us lost on short journeys, diverting us from life's major decisions is much easier.

After my mother's death, my father dropped me off at my grandparents' home and headed to Africa to work. He would return for short visits in the following years. Upon each visit, he would purchase gifts for our family and me. An electric guitar he bought for me became a way to reduce the loneliness that lived with me. I taught myself to play and eventually joined school friends for jam sessions. These sessions led to the creation of several rock bands. So far, this gift seemed innocent. It would soon open more harmful doors. Before I was fourteen, I had become proficient with the guitar and as a singer of rock and roll. Pride came to visit and convinced me that I was better than I was. Soon, I sat in with a local band of members older than myself. Even though I was not as skilled as they were, I began to travel with them. Marijuana was the first temptation, then LSD and other hallucinogens soon followed during my time with this musical group.

It was the 1960s, and Greer, South Carolina, did not yet have the Back Row culture. Our group heard of the place in Atlanta where you could walk the streets and openly ask for any drug you wanted. We made the trip to that street, and it was true. That part of Atlanta became our favorite destination. Later, it was also where I attempted to murder the heroin addicts. Principalities like this Atlanta street are assigned, Angels. Unseen battles rage for such sites. Had I the wisdom to predict the presence of Evil on those streets, I might have spotted the trouble traps set for my future. However, I did not, and I also did not realize that these streets grew more evil after each visit. I have traveled back to this area recently, and evidence exists that sin has lost that ground to the forces of Good. What a battle that must have been.

Music is not always bad. Some songs have evil intentions and words, while others are sung on the streets of heaven. In my case, music opened the door to wrong places that nearly claimed my life several times. This area of Atlanta became one of my earliest wrong turns. The men and women were not from the local Christian church on these streets. The influencers I chose to listen to were not singing healthy songs, nor was I. Instead, my reputation as a locally talented entertainer evolved into that of a violent drug dealer. You need to understand that a prime goal of the fallen one himself is to spot a happy future and ruin it. Could I have become blessed in the music world? Yes, maybe, but I chose poorly. The same was also true for sports. I might have had a future there, but this lifestyle replaced it. I can also testify that skills in music and sports frightened the fallen Angel, and he started a campaign to distract me toward other places.

Still, second chances came. Fast forward to my twenty-first birthday. One of my previous band members gave me a party. As a gift, he spiked a water jug with a lot of PCP. I was not fond of PCP, and he knew it. Later, we had words over his birthday present. The point is that you can't trust anyone in the world of drugs and unhealthy music. Death is always nearby, waiting on your mistakes.

Trusting a drug-doing friend with your future is not wise. After drinking his concoction, I nearly hit a tree head-on at high speed. It was not the only time I drove while under the influence. I never saw those angels of hope, but they were present and wrestling with their evil counterparts for my life. Who can you trust if you can't trust a friendly drug user or drug dealer? I got yet another second chance but was not ready to start over. Distractions blinded me. Too many of my friends did not get a second chance during those days. The evil agent named Drug Abuse claimed childhood friends and new acquaintances alike.

A few of them survived but became walking zombies due to those days of drug abuse. Loss comes in many forms and can last a lifetime.

Visits to Victor United Methodist ended, and so did my ability to think clearly. I ignored healthy life coaches and instead gravitated toward those who made poor decisions as I did. I replaced the blessed leadership and love with back-row losers like me. I closed the doors to healthy choices when I decided that church was not for me. I became comfortable with my drug-using replacements for the church friends at Victor United Methodist. I traded worship music for the worship of music.

The healthy life coaches did persist. But they had to do so from a distance. Thankfully, they knew how to pray intercessory prayers. Without them, I would not have survived. Today, I hope to be a fraction as effective as they were. One life coach was South Carolina Trooper Robert J. McCrary. He was a member of Victor United Methodist who showed me mercy rather than arresting me for several traffic tickets that I did not and could not pay. He and others prove that once you pull away from the good side, it does not pull away from you. There was a time when I hid from officers like Trooper McCrary. Today, I would love to thank him for who he was. Today, he is on my all-time hero list.

This man of the law showed me mercy. But, I continued to fear and resent the police for many years. Today, I see that a major war against law officers exists. The intensity of this battle should illustrate to all of us that Satan fears the police. If he fears them so much, friends of peace and hope should eagerly embrace them. At the time, I did not see intercession from people like Trooper McCrary as a chance to start over. I had welcomed a strong enemy named Stubbornness into my life. The evil enemy in charge of distractions works overtime to hide such intercession.

Others from that church family never gave up on me. They were determined. Determination is good, and Stubbornness is not. They gave me more than a second chance. Many Victor United Methodist members continued on a path of hope for much of their lives. I find this no coincidence. Still, I did not choose to become a Christian during those days. Today, I see many friends like Trooper McCrary, whose Christian integrity has passed down to their children and grandchildren. Those doors are the ones to step through.

We all must make a list of healthy choices and follow them wisely. Had I made a list of each path my early music choices would follow, I might have chosen differently. Music did come back and plays a beautiful role in my life and ministry today. But for a time, I stubbornly followed the wrong musical roads.

Sometime in my youngest years, I learned to be stubborn. I lost my balance and let Stubbornness convince me that my bad choices should continue. Be alert. Stubbornness is the name of a powerful hostile force. It blinded me into thinking that my musical skills qualified me to push away the hand of reason. It also closed other doors that I should have gone through instead. We should all be aware of our weaknesses and work to strengthen them. Stubbornness does not seem like evil to many people. For me, it was a blinding force.

The forgiving of my traffic tickets was not luck. It was a chance for a fresh start.

Dealing with Fear

I n my teen years, Fear was a leader among my enemies. Its force was so strong that it worked against me though I didn't realize it existed. Still, there came a time when I knew that change had to come. Something felt wrong. Pick a quiet place, turn off your phones and distractions, and think about each life-changing decision you made. Also, think about those that are ahead. Then accept that you have outside influences standing by to help or hurt you on each decision. Somehow, amid my mistakes, I knew that a significant change had to happen in my life. The Life Coaches in my path caused embedded that into my being.

By the time I entered high school, I was a good athlete, better than most. My grandfather saw that I played in all types of organized youth sports. He knew involving me with other boys and the team coaches would be good. But music influenced me most, and I drifted away from sports and into the world of drugs. Instead of playing in high school sports, I chose the drug culture. I replaced physical fitness with mental weakness. Maybe it was the influence of the good people I encountered or divine intercession, but something inside me knew I needed to make a drastic change. My studies also suffered. I failed English in the tenth grade and had to repeat that grade. I failed not because of my inability to understand. Instead, it was because of my desire not to do the work. Distractions turned my attention away from studying. Distractions ruled my thoughts. Getting a GED and entering the military was suggested during a counseling session with the Greer High school nurse, Mrs. Gordon, and Mrs. Hayes, the school guidance counselor.

At age seventeen, I graduated high school with that GED and tested for the Army and the Air Force. My aptitude scores for the Army were weak, but I had a high rank in electronics on the Air Force test. Today I have been in the field of electronics for over fifty years. That test result would impact my life and family for several generations. I knew nothing about electronics; Today, I know that the score had the hand of our Lord on it. That was yet another chance at a solid future coming from heaven. I did not believe in heavenly intercession at the time, only luck. Stubbornness still ruled my thoughts.

If you made a list, would you list any miracles that happened? If not, go back and add them. Then list their origin. Did you record any lousy advice that pointed you down the wrong path? Be honest. In my list, I see Fear as an unwelcomed visitor. I see Fear as a force that diverted my course down some troubled roads. I also realized battles fought for me during those days were not seen. The hidden enemy named Fear was a force I dealt with often in my list. I must also add the events around this period that some outstanding Life Coaches teamed up to help me.

When I enlisted in the Air Force, it was during the Vietnam war. Even though that war was raging and there was a draft, I had no fear of joining the military. Instead, I wanted to go to Vietnam to fight. Fighting had become my way of navigating my fear. On the surface, I had the reputation of being fearless. In truth, I was living in fear. My past childhood haunted me. I had nightmares of those days returning. The possibility of dying in the war had no impact, but returning to my past life did. I had to get away, far away, and Vietnam was possible if I joined the military.

Before discussing my time in the USAF, I will discuss fear more. Fear fueled my desire to hurt and kill in the Vietnam war. I thought that fear only worked one way, and I believed I could use Violence to fight off my worries. But the reputation I had built hurt others near me, others I did not want to scare or intimidate. Years later, at a funeral I preached for one of my younger Stewart cousins, I learned of the damages my reputation of violence had carelessly inflicted on others. After the service, two female cousins advised me that I gave them nightmares throughout their youngest years. They shared that they feared I would arrive at their home and hurt them and all their family members. Was this what members of my own family thought of me? During their years of fear, I was thirteen to seventeen. I never knew what my own family thought of me until that day. That reputation of Evil kept itself completely hidden from even me. Hidden Evil is predictable, but the damage it does is not. Distraction is the name of a potent agent of Evil that claimed too many victories over me. What I built inside myself as a defense mechanism also impacted others. Be very careful with fear. It is not the name of an agent Angel from Heaven.

Reputations can be good or bad. I worked to build a tough guy's reputation, but I never planned to hurt or scare these girls. Ladies, please forgive me. Despite my evil influence, you turned out well. You are products of generational blessings. I impacted you when I walked with companions of Evil. The evil agent named Fear and his brother named Violence stand close by us, spreading their misery even past a time when Peace replaces them in our hearts.

I went into the Air Force but left behind the fear of me. The choices we make often last a lifetime. We do not always know of the damage we do to others. My choice to become a tough guy delivered pain and fear to others. Their stories were not the only ones I would hear. Years after my time in the Air Force and after I was a Christian, My wife Kim's brother Mike Lemmons told me that Tim, an acquaintance, had spent time in a mental hospital over a similar fear of me. That story was even more of a shock. It happened when a close friend of his had an issue I dealt with physically. His friend had cheated me out of some money. The way I coerced him to pay me was wrong, and the story spread again that I was dangerous. The damage we do can last years past when we find peace.

Tim and I had previously had a relationship that I thought was healthy. We had no issues between us. But somehow, my reputation fueled a fear trigger in him. He spent considerable time in rehab because of me. Years later, I would run into him at a local store. I could tell that this chance meeting scared him again. Occasionally when I meet past acquaintances, I am asked if I am still a "hothead." And sadly, other old friends and family members still avoid me. The damage we do in life can cause ripples that go past our intentions. Fear can also cause permanent damage that may never go away, no matter how hard we work to repair it. Permanent damage like this is a living nightmare sent by the fallen angel. I own this mistake and many others like it made to others I encountered. Tim and too many others will never forget me as evil. Without forgetting the past, forgiveness suffers.

My early years in my grandmother's "Garden of Eden" home taught me peace, love, happiness, and beauty, but this was a short season. The fruit of this learning caused the evil agents to regroup only for a while. They would return with reinforcements by age fourteen, bringing some new and stronger soldiers. Hopelessness grew, and Hurt arrived. Rage would have great success with me and soon was promoted in rank because of this success against me. Anger took up residence in my soul and lived there for years. He worked on my branding as "Evil Me" permanently. During my time in my grandparents' home, I created the fear of me in my cousins. I do not push the blame for my transgressions onto unseen enemies. Instead, I know I opened each door where they entered my life. But once inside, they grew in strength. This fact makes me more determined to alert others of their presence. Even in the most protected of homes, Evil stands nearby. He does exist, and he does have a lot of allies. However, they cannot enter through closed doors. A study of my life proves they live, and there is hope, even for the most hopeless.

In the case of the enemy named Fear, he is among the most cunning. He fooled me often, but he lost his grip when I became a Christian. From that day until now, I know who wins the final battle. I am no longer afraid and strive to bring others out of the dark and into the light.

I wish that those I offended in my evil days would forgive me. Give me a second chance; Jesus has.

Keeping My Lunch Money

I t is wise to study ways to strengthen the walls of our fortresses. It is wise to know when an enemy is attacking. It is also wise to know where they will shoot at us. Violence had a powerful presence in my life. When and where did he enter my fortress? A structural evaluation of the strengths of the walls in our lives can better analyze how the enemy plans to break in.

My father originally built the store building beside my grandmother's home as a place where my grandmother could sell flowers that she grew. Her home and grounds radiated beauty and were also mighty fortresses of peace. Strong angels guarded the doors until I weakened one of those doors. After she retired, she sold the flower shop to a family who opened it as a small grocery store. It also had a kitchen where I enjoyed chili cheeseburgers and hot dog plates. Often grandmother would give me fifty cents to spend there. This purchase was my first experience with money. Keeping that money began the process of punching holes through the walls of her heavenly place of peace.

Living within walking distance of the store, boys lived in dysfunctional homes where violence had an accepted presence. Just outside the most protected of our homes lives enemies like this. Some of these boys would become a part of the most violent days of my future years. Some of these continued their dysfunctional lives until their death. These boys were products of generational curses, and so was I. But I had my spiritually healthy grandparents and other healthy life coaches.

We learn to deal with violence by watching those who care for us deal with it in their lives. It is a learned behavior that usually leads to future pain, imprisonment, and death if not taught correctly. These were the final destinations of too many of these young men. Imprisonment and death also called for me more than once.

There was a crossroads decision that I needed to make on how to keep my fifty cents of chili cheeseburger money. I took the wrong turn. Always nearby was my grandfather, who could have easily shared how to avoid becoming violent. I did not seek his counsel. Instead, I listened to the voice of Rage. Rage is so loud that it can drown out the voice of reason. I am not happy with this part of my story. I tell it as a study of the point in time when I would learn such a horrible lesson.

Fighting became a companion outside the guarded gates of my grandmother's haven of peace. Fistfights were one of the ways Violence expressed his outrage. The peace I found at Grandmother's home was under attack, and I didn't even know it. I had to fight often. It started with my desire to keep my fifty cents. Fighting became a regular part of my being, and it was the same for those boys around me. So, yes, I learned to defend myself the hard way. And yes, I gained a violent reputation accordingly. Soon, I could keep my fifty cents against older and much bigger boys. I quickly learned not to fight fair; I became very good at being very violent.

Winning fights using unfair tactics was how I gained my reputation. It became known that I would fight a bigger bully and attack from the shadows to even the score of a previously lost battle. I learned the element of surprise that some call sucker punching. In this, I became very good at being very bad. I also became more explosive and unpredictable. This evil trait followed me as I returned to the sanctuary of peace at Grandmother's home. Places of peaceful refuge are constantly under attack. The good news is that the Lord God has already assigned protective Angels to such sites. Jesus has appointed them to guard and protect us. Yes, they help us. While we are not to worship them, I certainly appreciate them. The duties assigned to Angels may have been a critical reason that one of the most potent Angels rebelled against God. Satan did not want to serve humanity. Instead, his pride wanted him to rule over us. A third of the other Angels agreed. Today, they secretly walk around us, hoping to ruin the joy and blessings due to children of the Lord Jesus Christ (Eph. 6:12; Ps. 34:7; 2 Pet. 2:4)

In the ground war between Good and Evil, several targets become under attack simultaneously. I added Fighting, Rage, and Violence to my list of bad choices, all on the same day. Even minor fighting reasons can turn our lives toward far more dangerous roads. Be on guard against even the smallest of reasons to be violent. At no time is the enemy named Violence a force of Good.

War does not always start with a significant show of force. Minor battles impacted my life for years, but each ensuing battle grew more evil. Early on in the campaign, Anger arrived. During these days of my life, I should have noticed such evils as enemies. Instead, I allowed them to divert me away from my protected place of refuge.

Be alert that places of peace are known as targets for the attacks of Satan. He knows they propagate second chances.

Starting Over

needed a fresh start; leaving my current culture and joining the United States Air Force was my doorway. After entering, I got some attention from the USAF leaders, who labeled me mature for seventeen years. They were wrong, but this label was part of the Lord Jesus's plan for my future. His plan continued when I moved to Electronics school and was promoted to the role of "Red Rope." My duties then included managing over 100 other Air Force students. Twenty months later, at my permanent duty station at Shaw Air Force base in Sumter, South Carolina, I was promoted to sergeant well ahead of others who had far more years of service than me. People believed in me, but I had yet to believe in myself or have hope for a productive future. The leadership role that an earlier Life Coach Mr. Smiley Williams had trusted me with was growing.

While in Electronics school at Keesler AFB in Biloxi, Mississippi, I used my temporary leadership duties to bully others. I ruled more with my fists and mouth than with any leadership abilities, and fear was still my influence of choice. One night, a knock came on my door. A group of Airmen invited me to a prayer meeting they were holding upstairs. They stated that my name was on their hearts. I scolded and threatened them and sent them on their way. Minutes later, a larger group came with the same invitation. This time I accepted. Moments later, I accepted Jesus as my Savior.

My support group changed from others like me to men of prayer and worship. My ability to see more clearly significantly increased. I prayed for forgiveness of my past sins and the wisdom to see more clearly during this time. I was finally starting over.

The fallen Angel Satan launched a major campaign to stop my forward march at this crossroad. As a Christian, you can expect this. However, you can also expect a more significant, robust protection force to march onto the battlefields ahead of you. Wisdom was soon to arrive to begin its plan to clear my thoughts. I can't say that I prayed for learning at this stage, but someone in my life had sent up prayers for just such an arrival.

Before I proceed, here is a word of caution. Along the roads you will follow as a Christian, you will meet people of solid integrity that will guide you wisely. Life coaches with good intentions will appear. So will False Prophets. They will come into your life with smiles, pats on the back, and promises of support and protection. Be careful. Some are sent by the Evil One and will appear in your lives as people claiming to be your friend.

A fresh start had arrived. Now I knew that I had to distance myself from my past. Quickly, I began to see more clearly. A few men I previously trusted tried to lure me back into their circle of recent sin. One of them admitted to being a Witch and even demonstrated some scary and evil skills I never knew he had. Soon his attempts to lure him away from life as a Christian included more like him, who were Witches, and some were also Satanists. The war to take me away from a healthy future found a higher gear. Evil chose to come out of hiding. Men I would have fought for before I became a Christian had revealed their true character. My ability to see more clearly improved. The gift of such wisdom was unexpected.

I realized that I was about to flunk out of Electronics School. My roommate was Mr. Ed Golka. He was not a fan of me or my lifestyle. However, he offered to tutor me through some material, and I graduated. People like him were always nearby, but evil did an excellent job distracting me from seeing them. Thanks, Mr. Golka; you are now on my list of all-time heroes. I wonder how many others like him I ignored in my past with an outstretched hand? I now realize that a plan exists to rob us of the wisdom offered by Life Coaches.

When given the role of leader, it was out of place. I had not earned such a role. Today I see those roles as a part of a lifelong plan to write this book. Be alert for unlikely blessings in your life. They may be part of another larger plan for your future. Put such gifts down on the list you should keep of things in your life. They will prove helpful later. It took some extra effort from humans and Good Angels alike, but I had finally started over. The fallen one knows what can happen if he leaves Christians alone. I should have expected that he would set new trouble traps. His goal was to remove my support group. Young Christians must, and I emphasize firmly, have a support group like those available at the local Christian church near you.

Another point to consider is that chance encounters with people can be meaningful, even if you have had only a few meetings with them. Don't just focus on your closest circles of friends for good advice. God will send you many crossing guards that may only stand at a single crossroads turn. One such encounter came while I was on Keesler AFB. One night as I drove onto the base through the main gate, I noticed an Airman being attacked just outside our grounds by a group of local thugs. I rushed to help him and saw another Airman running to the rescue. Together we overcame the thugs. This other "rescuer" was Ulysses Frontha. I could have missed many train wrecks if I had spent more time with people like Ulysses and Ed Golka. Stay alert to crossing guards like them. They may only show up to offer guidance once, but their impact can change your life. Someone in your life's journey needs your input if you are such a man. They need your wisdom.

Ed Golka was instrumental in giving me a fresh start. Ulysses Frontha was instrumental in showing me how to channel my physical skills to help others.

Ulysses Frontha

Moving Back to South Carolina

My next move was to my permanent duty station at a base near my home in South Carolina. Once there, I realized that Air Force leadership planned to move me quickly through their ranks. Maybe, a move to a base near my home was a part of their plan to do that. Or, perhaps it was a reward for my early efforts to be a member of the Air Force special ops group known as Pararesuce, AKA PJ. Whatever the reason, I was now leaving my Christian support group and headed back to a place too close to my old habits.

As a PJ recruit, I wanted to become a trained killer. The Air Force's purpose for its Pararecsue men was to rescue downed pilots behind the lines in Vietnam. When an injury took me out of PJ training and into Electronics school, I volunteered to go to Vietnam instead. However, the Lord had other plans for me. Upon graduating from Electronics school, I volunteered for Vietnam again. All of the others in my class went to Vietnam. I was the only one sent to a base near home.

I improved my fighting skills at Air Force Boot camp, PJ indoctrination, and Shaw Air Force Base. Boxing gloves became a common way to settle disagreements. My bare-knuckled street skills blossomed into gloved-hand victories. Gambling on matches was common. I weighed 155 pounds, an unfilled weight in competition boxers on my stationed bases. So, I competed. We could suddenly be on a private plane for an unofficial boxing trip. Any victories went into the pockets of others and not into mine. There was no extra pay for being on a boxing team, even for one like me, who won most of the time. Instead, I was the Golden boy of my weight class for a time, with my reward only being a brushed face or busted nose.

In a short time after my new assignment to Shaw AFB, I began to visit my home in Greer, SC, every weekend. I am unclear if my Shaw AFB assignment was a reward or a curse. I do know that more battles for my future began with this move. My fresh start came under a fierce attack. I suggest to all my readers that you can often measure the trueness of your course in life by the amount of opposition to it. When the road you travel has many detours, your original destination threatens the Fallen One's plans. This move to a base near home would eventually fill with blessings. But first, I would lose many battles, some of which came with a bloody nose.

Upon making sergeant, I gained new adversaries at Shaw AFB. Making that rank early made many airmen with more years in service than myself angry. I was looking for my next support group of Christians. Instead, I found new enemies. In all fairness, I ignored Christians at my duty station. This error was strike one in my turn at bat. My Division was a wartime readiness unit, trained to deploy and maintain a communications system to call in an F4 Fighter strike. I now had a permanent assignment. Our staff was large enough to send entire teams to any location for a fighter strike worldwide.

My rank allowed me to assign duties to other lower-ranked Airmen. Then I could more often drive the two hours to my home place in Greer, South Carolina, and stay longer than a weekend. This responsibility was a blessing. I used it as a curse.

I usually won when boxing. Leaving the base on weekends often put me out of touch, and I missed several unscheduled, off-base, and off-record events that could include gambling on boxing matches. Missing matches by being off base did not keep me in good favor. My direct line of Air Force leaders were solid Life Coaches who did not participate in unsanctioned competitions or gambling. They tried to counsel me against these weekend activities. Many of them also advised me against being on this unsanctioned boxing team. I did not listen.

Losing one match against a Marine opponent over which I had two previous victories began my fall from grace. After that match, I was attacked by four Marines on the way to the parking lot. Over twenty of my fellow Airmen watched. One officer stopped them from helping me. That night I lost more than a match. That night further signaled my fall from grace and disconnected me from ever trusting the twenty who watched as I lost that parking lot brawl. Evil never plays fair.

I took advantage of my leadership role in the USAF. At that time in my life, I did not have integrity. At Shaw AFB, my previous support group was missing. The sergeants over me were all super-good leaders, and integrity ruled. They went about the business of Air Force leadership wisely. But, I did not join a Christian support group. Soon, I began more frequent and longer weekend travels to my homeplace. The Back Row called loudly to me.

My bedroom at my grandparents' home was still available, and they welcomed me. They prayed that my next time in their home would see a wiser and better-behaved Christian. However, my presence continued to give nightmares to my cousins. Fear followed me back to Greer. This time, I was even more capable of violence and more deserving of the fear they had of me. Others who doubted my conversion to Christianity rightfully did not welcome me. Soon the Back Row was my choice of home, and my grandmother's house was just a place to lay my head.

I have searched for the thinking that again put me on the local Back Row. Nothing comes to mind. Clutter saw to that. I share this to illustrate that we will not always spot the decisions that fuel our mistakes. Once we make a small step off-course, the following false steps become easier to take. Soon, we lose our way back to the beginning and fall victim to the lie that we must backtrack through each wrong turn to start over. I was a Christian. But, I was a back-slidden Christian. Soon, I was on a path that could erase efforts to give me a fresh start in life. At some point, our last rescue comes. I was dangerously unaware of that fact.

Sinners need not backtrack to obtain forgiveness. There is no need to retrace our steps. We must only believe in Christ Jesus, repent, and ask him for forgiveness. He has already paid for our sins. We do not need to and can not fix yesterday's mistakes. Here is the only path your need to follow. From the New King James Bible: *Romans 3:23, Romans 6:23, Romans 5:8, Romans 10:13.*

Also, remember that Jesus said he forgives our sins as far as the East is from the West. The East and the West never touch. So, please take this to mean that yesterday's sins are no longer held against us. Once he forgives us, we should move forward and release the past. He has. *Psalm 103: 11-12*

We are a factor in what and who we choose as our surroundings. I knew people of character, and I knew where to find them. People of solid Christian character like Chris Dumas, Carol Sims, Mimi Gordon, and others were still nearby. They had positively impacted my past, but I chose a different support group this time. Sadly, it was years before I even appreciated their influence on my life. I was ashamed of who I was and did not want to go around people of integrity. I lost track of the fact that Jesus forgives yesterday's sins and forgets them immediately.

Some on the Back Row still knew my reputation for violence. But, I had to rebuild it for others. That culture had changed a lot. Evil no longer hid as often and instead loudly displayed its influence. Another change was in drug use. Hallucinogens like LSD and Mescaline were no longer the most popular drug choice. While I had a lot of history using most drugs, I avoided using a syringe to shoot drugs. Fistfights returned, but now I had the skills to hurt people much worse. I could tell many stories about how the Back Row had changed. Instead, I will summarize by saying that such places fuel evil, and the Back Row has become far more deadly.

Soon, I was dealing drugs again. I chose to distance myself from those who depended on the needle. For a time, I used what little strength of character I had left as a Christian to promote against using such drugs to my brothers and sisters on the Back Row. Users began to seek me out to ask for help for their addictions. While my intentions may have leaned toward Good, I still snorted and sold cocaine myself. I still called Christ my Lord but fell deeper into the pits of misery with each snort.

Even as I was living intensely in sin, I became known as one who could help others on the Back Row overcome the use of needles. Strange as that may seem to some, numerous levels of dysfunction do exist. Not all drug users are one hundred percent evil. My distorted desire to help eventually cost me my career in the USAF.

Bob was a friend since high school with whom, years earlier, I had smoked pot. He had migrated to shooting drugs and approached me for help. My advice was for him to quit using. A few weeks later, he again asked for my help. I offered to take all his drugs with me while I returned to Shaw AFB for a week. I suggested forcing Bob to quit for a week, which would prove it possible to stop permanently. Even in this unrealistic promise of hope, I had another intent. I would smoke his pot until I returned it. He agreed, and I returned to Shaw AFB with his MDA bag and a large pot bag. This move was not the most brilliant move I made during those days. In my newly found desire to help others, I did not realize that you can't commit sinful things to solve problems.

On the late-night drive back to Shaw Air Force Base, I noticed a car on the side of the highway and a man flagging me down. I stopped and drove him thirty miles to a gas station for fuel and then back to his car. On the drive, he asked if I wanted to smoke one? He rolled one up, and we smoked it. Next, I opened Bob's big bag of marijuana and rolled us another one. He traveled on to Charleston, and I continued to Shaw AFB.

Later that week, he ratted me out to a Charleston detective. My rider was an informant. His Charleston, SC, detective called Shaw AFB police with my name and car's tag number. The Base Police searched me and found Bob's stash in my car and room. My intentions to help Bob turned into an undesirable discharge from the USAF. Before that day, I had been loyal not to take drugs on Shaw AFB. I used no wisdom in my desire to help Bob. With this twisted kind of value system, a train wreck was imminent. I offer the lesson that trying to hold onto good intentions when living in sin is impossible. My only time to have drugs in my room at the base was predictably dumb. That one time was all it took for Evil to claim a victory.

It only takes one false step to get caught in a trouble trap forever. My desire to help someone in my back-row support group went wrong. That one-time instance had spiritual warfare written all over it. The trap was set, and I fell for it, specifically into it. Had I only given the Charleston informant a ride that night and not offered to smoke dope with him, my life in the USAF would have continued.

As a Christian, I was under attack. I quickly lost track of my promises. I had not yet spent enough time in praise, worship, and Bible study. Had I done so, I would have wholly dodged these trouble traps and quickly embraced the Christian support groups at Shaw AFB. However, my future was still under the care of my Father, Jesus. No matter how many mistakes I made, the wrong roads I chose to follow, and how many evils worked against me, my Lord still had me in His hands. I missed that a two-hour drive to my home was the plan to provide me with a Christian support group. Instead, I parked my new car in the Back Row, not near Church's parking lot.

Regret is the name of a fallen Angel. Turning our sins over to the Lord Jesus Christ for his forgiveness erases regret. Today, I am where he wanted me to be. I have the family, friends, and support groups he planned for me. There is no regret. I rejoice in where I am.

Each one of us makes mistakes. My Air Force leadership put up with a lot from me. What happened to my Air Force career was planned as a tool that would one day place me right where I was supposed to be. I have no regrets and hold no grudges. Each of my USAF leaders is still on my hero list. I own the mistakes that I alone made. Today, there are no better careers for young people than the USAF. Integrity and discipline abound in the USAF. However, I had neither of these traits at Shaw AFB.

Life coaches have invested time in me, but I ignored their outstretched hands. Trooper McCrary's mercy aided my desire to be a servant of law and order one day. Sadly, I only knew this too late to thank him in person. My roommate at electronics tech school, Ed Golka, taught me that education is key to our future. Ulysses Frontha taught me the correct way to help others in need. For a time, I ignored life coaches like these men. At the time they interacted with my life's journey, I did not see the impact their guidance would have on my life.

My desire to help Bob wrongly included my desire to smoke some of his pot. I offer this story to illustrate that my plan to help included a hidden evil trap that got me. Trying to help a fellow human is admirable. How close you get to their problem can be a risk. I learned this the hard way.

Learning to spot healthy helping hands in real-time is challenging. Looking back, I see more clearly than I did back then. Today, I see many life events built toward a bigger plan for my future than I realized. More specifically, another life was on a journey that would intersect with me permanently. That life was my wonderful wife, Kim Lemmons Stewart. While I could not see her for years to come, a plan was in place to unite us one day in the future. Once we joined, my blessings matured. More importantly, the plan for our descendants began. This plan continues throughout eternity. The evil master of destruction does not have this future.

When I was moving back into South Carolina, Kim moved from her home in California to my hometown of Greer, SC. Destiny is hard to realize while riding the roads alongside a terrible choice of companions. But, Destiny is the name of a powerful agent of the Lord Jesus. Destiny had already begun paving the streets of hope for me. Kim was to be my reward soon.

Don't get stuck on the road to destruction. Second chances can and do evolve into fresh starts.

Jail Time

I did not spend any time in Air Force jail yet. An attorney was assigned to me, and I returned to my duties. However, the following weekend, I traveled back to the Back Row. Bob never got his drugs back, overdosed, and died a short time later. Such was life on the Back Row. Such was my ability to see clearly.

I was called into the office for some talks back on the base. My sergeants offered constructive advice that went in one ear and out. Leadership made phone calls to my grandparents, and I burdened them again. A plan was underway to get me some time to recover at their home. This offer of help I abused. I began to spend more days in the Back Row. My absence at the base appeared to be their way of getting an undesirable Airman out of their hair. When I asked if I needed a pass to leave for a while, the advice was that I did not. I misused that freedom, and it would one day cost me.

Soon, I was dealing more drugs on the Back Row and threw caution to the wind. The Greer Police Department used a Back Row informant to introduce over thirty dealers to an undercover agent who made drug buys from us, including me. I don't know when or what I sold because I sold a lot of dope to anyone who asked. My trips from the Back Row back to Shaw AFB became less frequent. I learned of the undercover drug buys on the Back Row and that I had a warrant for my arrest pending. I parked in the Back Row and waited. Soon, a pickup truck with two plain-clothed officers arrived, handcuffed me, and delivered me in the bed of that truck to jail. Days later, I was transported to the Greenville County Jail for several weeks while waiting on the Air Force police to pick me up. They did arrive but took me to Fort Gordon, Georgia, to their Federal Disciplinary Barracks as a military deserter.

Technically I was arrested on a weekend in Greer, South Carolina, and could not be a deserter. The false charge was a tactic by upper leadership to get my attention. Maybe my fall from being the golden boy contributed to these decisions. Whatever the reason, I learned what a military jail is all about. Months later, I was picked up at Fort Gorden by the Shaw base police and taken back to Shaw. The charges as a deserter were dropped. At this time, I had not yet had my first conversations with my USAF attorney. So, I awaited my trial for possession of someone else's drugs. Curiously I saw a change of heart from some of my leadership at Shaw. They offered to help me get my life together. I was wisely counseled and, as a result, felt some hope. My grandparents back in Greer were brought into the conversations again and asked if I could stay there for a prolonged time to get my head straight and wait on my USAF trial. A Master Sergeant counseled me I was undesirable on Shaw AFB until I was cleared of any criminal charges. I misinterpreted that to mean I could go home forever. Living in sin is often accompanied by a lack of sound judgment. You can also count on sin to rob you of sound comprehension.

I also learned that the attorney I had yet to see or talk with claimed that my search was unlawful because the informant in Charleston did not qualify for a search warrant at Shaw AFB. He was preparing to defend me on illegal search grounds. Years later, when I was a Greer, South Carolina police officer myself, I learned that he would have been right, and my case would have resulted in a dismissal of all charges. Still, I knew that upper leadership felt I was undesirable to them. They were correct—maybe not legally correct, but morally right. I did not have the integrity inherent in those wearing the USAF uniform.

It was suggested that I return to my grandparents' home and wait on a call to return for my trial. It sounded good to me. I went home to follow that advice. No calls came asking me to return to the base. Once again, I incorrectly thought that my undesirability authorized my absence on the base and that I would get a call from the attorney when I should return. No phone calls or mail from Shaw AFB came once I returned to Greer. My grandfather called Shaw AFB leadership several times, only to be told to be patient.

So, I took it on myself to go back to Shaw AFB. When I arrived, my room at the barracks was empty, and all my possessions were gone, including an autographed Atlanta Braves baseball by Hank Aaron and the entire team. I rushed to one of my sergeants' offices. He panicked, said I should leave the base immediately, and warned me that I would "be arrested on sight." When asked why? He commented that it was out of their hands. Who were they? My immediate leadership had counseled me contrary to what I was hearing now. Contrary orders must have come down from above. I left and returned to Greer. Further calls to the base went unanswered.

Something did eventually come in the mail. It was an undesirable discharge, claiming that I had been AWOL. I was due some discipline, but this was a poor way for them to get rid of me without a trial. It was an easy way out for them. A call to the base did result in a first and only conversation with the attorney appointed for me. He stated he did not like what happened and was preparing a case for an illegal search because the Charleston informant had no credibility on Shaw AFB and the subsequent investigation was unlawful. But, the discharge changed everything he was planning.

In summary, I was undoubtedly involved in illegal and immoral things. I was certainly undesirable. I got what I deserved.

These lost days in my life evolved into me being right where I am supposed to be, doing exactly what I am supposed to do, with the people I was to do it with. I have no regrets. Today, I claim to be a veteran and love my country. I have considered asking for a final hearing to change my discharge to at least a general rating. Yes, that scar still hurts, but Christ still has nail-scarred hands, so I can tolerate mine.

I offer that joining the military made me a better man and came into my life when I needed the discipline and guidance I learned there. It turned my desire to be violent and fight into a trade as an electronics troubleshooter that began in 1972. That entire process was in the hands of my Lord Jesus. He had a plan and countered every false step I made and every trouble trap set for me. I have no regrets today and pray that readers will consider a role in the United States military as I did.

My charge for distributing PCP soon came up for a preliminary hearing in Greer, South Carolina. When I arrived in court that day, to my surprise, my dear aunt Audrey Stewart Rector was there. All of us facing distribution charges were also there. Few had an attorney, and I did not either. I was ready to plead guilty instead. One of the other drug dealers had hired the famous defense attorney Jack Lynn. I knew that I could not hire him or anyone else. I did notice my aunt Audrey speaking with him privately and wondered what she was saying. When they called my name and asked if I had an Attorney, Jack Lynn stood up as my counsel. Somehow Aunt Audrey had secured him to defend me.

I would later learn that she explained my troubled youth and added my future potential to contribute to society with my electronics education. Jack Lynn agreed that I was worthy of his help. Aunt Audrey was my Angel more than once. Attorney Jack Lynn was now on my team. He is also on my all-time list of heroes. While writing this book, I reached out to Jack to thank him. I had not spoken to him for over forty-six years. He commented that he did nothing. Instead, he desired to get people to work toward a better future independently. Jack, Sir, you're mistaken.

Without you, I would not be writing this book of hope and salvation today. You were a significant life coach in my journey through life. Your wisdom will undoubtedly provide hope to readers of this book. Another attorney of similar character that I know today is Matt Henderson. Matt is an excellent Attorney but is also a solid Christian friend. He and Jack Lynn proved to be examples of life coaches whose help can divert our lives' directions in powerful ways.

After this hearing, dates for our trials followed. When the trial date came, most of us received time in prison, with very few getting probations. I was an exception. I received two years' probation, a hefty fine to pay, and a mandate to get and keep the same job for those two years. I would be granted a "conditional discharge" of all my criminal records if I completed the terms of my probation. At my sentencing, the judge asked the courtroom deputy to come to the front and advised me that I could even wear the same agency uniform that he was wearing if I finished my conditions. Few believed that I would follow through. Aunt Audrey prayed, and I remembered what that judge said.

On paper, I received a conditional discharge. In reality, I received the benefit of heavenly intercession. Why? I struggled with this answer for years. I knew that I needed a lifestyle change when I was seventeen. I knew this civilian discharge and my military discharge had a purpose that I would eventually realize. But, I had some dues to pay first. And I had rebuilding pending as well.

Once again, Many thanks to Aunt Audrey and Attorney Jack Lynn. These heroes were all about second chances and fresh starts. As unlikely as it seems, today, I call Veterans, Police Officers, Local and National Politicians, Attorneys, and Judges my personal friends.

I received an undesirable discharge from the Air Force and a conditional discharge from a civilian judge in one year. When the

Lord Jesus is on our side, anything is possible. There is always hope for the most hopeless of souls.

Strange how the USAF discharge and the one for my criminal charges would eventually evolve into blessings. Second chances can start after bad decisions.

Living Through My Sentence

heard the judge say I could become a police officer one day. But, it would be years before I remembered this promise. I offer that this is true for any of us. Often we hear of the promise of a bright future but don't start working toward it. Far too early in our life of sin, we quit believing in hope. This mistaken belief is very true for criminals and noncriminals. Robbing us of hope is an effective battle plan of the enemy, Satan. I did not think that this future would ever be possible in my case. I was wrong. I serve a risen Saviour who came back from death. With him, anything is possible.

As a backslidden Christian, I was already living with conviction, not the type that would put me behind bars, but another more intense conviction. There were expectations for what I was to do in my life as a Christian. When I refused to do so, I sentenced myself to personal imprisonment, which hurt. That pain ate at me at every decision. That small, quiet voice had become very loud. I decided to move away from my life in the Back Row, but the enemy named Loneliness returned once I began that move.

I struggled to battle with him and prayed for help. The answer came when I began to enjoy my times on the Back Row less and less. Fights still came, but I no longer enjoyed my victories and began to suffer new losses. Death came closer and closer each time, wanting to claim me as his prize. And finally, I saw his hand. His desire to gloat worked against him. I searched my past more often and spotted countless times when he was present, pushing me toward misery—laughing and rejoicing at his victory over me. Being eternally saved, he knew that he could not change that. His response to the lord's children is an attempt to punish us while we live on this side of glory. For a time, he met his goals with me.

For those who do not choose Jesus, the enemy's goal to spread misery can evolve into eternal pain. For Christians, He can only work to reduce our earthly peace, hope, and joy. I finally had enough of this and decided to take steps toward who the Lord Jesus was calling me to be. At the time, I did not know I would preach or write a book one day. I only knew that I was tired of being beaten down. Being obedient is essential to realizing the earthly blessings that Christians can have. Discipline was not a friend of mine. I realized that this must change.

At the beginning of my criminal sentence, I went to work. It was not in electronics. Instead, I made furniture. That job taught me the value of hard work, which has served me well. But learning to do hard work was not the only thing planned for my time at this job. It also introduced me to Gail Petree, a previous high school friend. Gail would soon introduce me to what would become her sister-in-law and my future wife, Kimmy Lemmons. There are often twists and turns on the journey to the blessings ahead for Christians. This twist would open the door to peace and joy beyond measure. Be on the lookout for such intervention in your life's journey. Don't let hard work distract you from seeking treasures planned for you while on the job. Don't rush to change careers when discipline and hard work are required.

1978: Kim's Brother Mark Lemmons, Wife Gail
Petree Lemmons, and son, Bradley

Soon, I had an encounter with Kim (Kimmy). My old friend, Mike Lee, was dating her cousin, Tootsie Cox. When I spotted the three of them at a convenience store, I immediately knew Kim would be my future. But I let them drive away without asking for a date. I was still a back-row thug and felt she would not be attracted to me anyway. I prayed over this encounter and asked for another. Soon, I visited a local hangout and spotted Kim and a girlfriend inside. I already had two back-row-type girls with me. I spoke to Kim and learned that they needed a ride home. I quickly put the other two girls in the back seat and Kim in the front seat beside me. I took the other two girls home first, then Kim and her girlfriend. This time, I asked her for a date. She said yes.

On our first date, I arrived at her house and waited downstairs with her father, Clarence (Al) Lemmons, for her to come downstairs. Al was cleaning the biggest handgun I had ever seen. He advised me that he was recently retired from the US Navy. Besides that comment, Al Lemmons spoke no other words. He only stared me down and continued to clean his gun. When Kim finally came down, she was breathtaking and well worth the wait I had with her father. His last words were to tell me to have her home by 10:30 p.m. and not do anything I would not do if he were in the back seat.

I knew from that night that Kim was my future. The lure of the Back Row weakened, and the desire to be a better man grew. My road to the promised land had begun. I completed my probation, paid all my fines, kept my job, and gained my life partner. However, I did not expect a discharge of my criminal record. That fact had slipped my mind. And for a time, I ignored it.

The Back Row had been a frequent location to park and watch as my friends arrived. There, I stayed distracted and chose Clutter as my constant companion. I thought this environment made me happy. That thought was a monumental mistake. That was not happiness and instead was a victory against me from the master of misdirection. Today I see the traffic patterns more clearly than I did back then. Hope often rode through the Back Row, slowed, and opened the door for us to enter. But, I only saw this in my memories. I also see the forces that caused us to ignore him. Loneliness was always a powerful force in the Back Row. How could we be so lonely when with so many people present? We had Diversions and Distractions always nearby, and they used Addiction as their ally. Loneliness was possibly one of our greatest enemies. He hurt us so badly that it weakened our senses to the point where we more easily accepted dysfunctional lifestyles as comfort.

One great day, the battle for my future saw the forces of Good clear the Back Row of all enemies working against my destiny.

Strangely, but not coincidently, I was able to look just a few feet away from the Back Row to a place where my future would begin. I did not deserve even to know Kim's name at that time. But mercy saw things differently. That day, Hope rode past me on the Back Row, stopped, and Mercy, Peace, and Generational Blessings all jumped out and cleared the path for me to see across the road to where Kim was. Please don't miss similar battles raging in your life. Pay attention to road signs, crossing guides, and Distractions. Victory is always a possibility—always! There is hope for the hopeless. For me, it was just across the street.

Just across the road from the forces of Evil was my future. This experience was not just a second chance. It was my best chance.

Changes Came Fast

oon Kim and I were married. Al Lemmons disapproved of me and refused to support us. So, we eloped and were married by the same judge who officiated my drug-trafficking preliminary hearing, Mr. Carey Werner. We moved into a rented mobile home and started our family. Soon, I had a new electronics job in a local plastics manufacturing plant.

In 1976, our son Anthony was born; in 1978, our daughter Melanie was born. We had improved our financial income but had little to show. I had given up drugs, but drinking and smoking pot remained. How Kim put up with me is a testimony to the patience she learned from her precious mother. The Back Row was no longer a destination, but some old back-row friends came to our home to party instead.

During this time, a new enemy arrived at our house. It was Cash Flow. Today, that enemy attacks most married couples early. My lifestyle was proving that I could not manage money. This burden was what welcomed a new enemy into our lives. That enemy took on the role of Stress. It was the stress of not having enough resources to raise a family. The same enemy attacks young married couples often and fiercely. He welcomes his forces of Separation and Disagreement to join him in his attack against Harmony. Together they work towards a goal of Divorce.

I had not yet learned much about being a Christian and did not know how to pray very well. As a result, this stress gained a foothold in my family, which grew faster than our children. Talking to the Lord Jesus opens the door to improved hearing.

Dedicating time to pray improves our ability to hear the wisdom of the Holy Spirit. With the burden of stress filling our minds, we allow distractions to overwhelm our ability to listen to this gentile voice. There was nearby another resource nearby that taught me how to bear the burdens of starting a family. That place was Mt. Lebanon Baptist Church. Thinking that I could navigate these troubled roads of financial peace without a solid support group was a mistake.

The fallen one is winning a significant victory over young people. Evidence exists in the absence of young people in church families. From college age to around 40, the reduced numbers in attendance are noticeable. That fact alone proves that young families are and continue to be a target for his evil battle plans.

Among the many bad financial choices I made, I did make one wise move. I knew that the electronics world was moving toward microprocessors and spent our precious money to buy one of the earliest Apple computers ever sold. This move proved helpful in several ways. One of them was that I had to learn to write assembly language code required to get my Apple to do much of anything. Focusing on learning this skill forced me to reduce my pot and alcohol use. Simple little things like this can go unnoticed in our lives. But many small things come our way if we are wise enough to see their arrival.

Apple Serial # 15,925, Bought in 1979

While learning the world of computers, I made sacrifices that our family and friends thought were crazy. Years later, more than one of our family and friends told me that they thought my purchase proved that I was a fool. This sacrifice had the hand of our lord on it. Yes, it took greatly needed cash flow to purchase a computer. However, it also steered my time away from less healthy distractions and habits. I took that gamble blindly. But I did so in hopes that I could improve my families future with this education. It worked. Other unexpected fruitful changes came soon after.

Changing our directions does not always immediately lead to Hope's final destination. One such example came when the frequent visits to the Back Row evolved into parties at our home. We would set up a volleyball net, loudly play ball, drink, and smoke pot, all out in the open on weekends. We partied hard at such events. Some days, there were fifty or more people in our front yard. Kim's family has numerous homes near ours. Those relatives and neighbors passed by our house each Sunday while traveling to their local church, Mount Lebanon Baptist. We usually drank a couple of beer kegs while playing and did not try to hide it. We also smoked pot in the front yard and had boxing matches. We had moved the Back Row to this sacred neighborhood, and I was once again a pack leader. Our sins were noticeable and bothersome to this neighborhood. My bad reputation changed to one of a public partier and an idiot spending money on evil parties and stupid computers instead of investing in my family's future. I did not think about what the churchgoers thought. This lifestyle is typical of someone who is out of balance. I needed change to come soon. Healthy change. My family was at risk of following in my footsteps.

Mount Lebanon Baptist Church, 572 Mt. Lebanon
Church Road, Greer, SC 29651

Our reputation for evil deeds spread fast. But, something new happened. Our family started to get visits from a member of Mt. Lebanon Church, Mrs. Glenda Riley. She never condemned us or spoke harshly against our actions. Instead, she talked of Jesus and His Love for us. As a backslidden Christian, I could not push her away. Even though I tried, I doubt she would leave us alone anyway. The peace that she shared burdened me. I quickly became convicted again—this time more hurtful. Today I often pray for others lost in sin that convictions visit them as they did for me.

Praying that prayer is one of a righteous nature, one that the Lord Jesus wants to answer.

Mrs. Glenda Riley

But the parties continued, and my reputation grew darker. My children became acquainted with a sinful lifestyle I propagated at a young age. Soon, they began to ask questions about what I smoked (Kim and I did not smoke tobacco) and why I drank. The conviction grew. Still, I was not ready to change my ways. Just after Christmas in January 1981, a fire burned our mobile home, and we had no insurance. I was in the shower when I heard the explosion of our oil-fired furnace. Quickly and still naked, I evacuated our family outside and into a freezing January evening. I ran back into the now fully engulfed mobile home not to get a pair of pants but my Apple computer. Neighbors and family arrived, and one of them brought me some clothes. I asked our Lord why this happened to us and why I was naked? The word *humble* quickly came to mind. I was too proud and stubborn to respond to the conviction I had felt for a long time.

Since that day of humbling, I have stressed over similar events in the lives of people I love. Fire humbled me. Death has been a visitor that humbled others. I have asked why death comes to people who lead very fruitful lives. I have realized that some children of Jesus are called to their heavenly reward early as a humbling agents to others they loved. My precious grandson Colin may have been just such an example? I wonder? I miss him terribly. But I have some peace in something he told me. A few years before his passing, I pressed him to learn what he thought about Christ Jesus. He firmly told me, "Poppa, don't worry about me. I love Jesus and will be in Heaven one day"!

Has a loved one left you with precious memories? If you have lost a loved one that you are sure is now in heaven, do not make the mistake of becoming bitter over the loss. Instead, remember that a reunion is possible and treasure what they left behind. Plan a reunion. Let their eternal blessing become your reason for renewed peace in your life. Your journey to this destination may require a change.

After the fire, second chances, starting over, and fresh starts had a more impactful meaning. I worked as an electronics instrumentation troubleshooter at the Celanese plastics manufacturing plant in Greer, South Carolina, at the time. My fellow employees put together some cash for us. That was a welcomed blessing. But what happened next was unexpected. My cousins and Kim's families showed up with clothes, money, and food. They knew of my reputation, but they came to our rescue anyway. Humbleness set up a home inside my heart where I had never allowed him to enter. This drastic and attention-getting event was not just for me. It also illustrates to those who have given up on having hope for happiness that hope is always possible. That fire was for them and me. The fallen angel, Satan, uses many evil resources against us. Our Lord uses many as well. Humbleness, Conviction, and visitors from people like Mrs. Riley combined to put us where we needed to be. We lost material things, but we gained eternal blessings.

We moved into a room in the home of Kim's parents. Al Lemmons still did not approve of me, and rightly so. But her mother, Jewel Henson Lemmons, made a difference. Jewel also became the mother I had lost when I was nine years old. Jewel, my aunt Audrey Stewart Rector, my grandparents, and other cousins became lifelines to us in many ways. Sadly I only understood their value far too late.

While wondering how to have our own home again, the answer came from an unlikely place. It came from the people at Mt. Lebanon Baptist Church. Yes, it came from the people who drove by on the way to church and saw our sinful actions in our front yard for the preceding two years. They knew who we were and what we were doing. But, they showed up in force and replaced our clothes, brought food, gave money, and even replaced the Christmas toys our young children had lost. Humility was a new and unexpected friend. We still needed a home, and the Mt. Lebanon family was not through. Mrs. Georgia Sloan offered us a house to move to our lot next door to Kim's parents. We paid less for the home than the cost of moving it. I find it no coincidence that the total cost was close to the gifts of cash we had just received. Years later, I would become a volunteer leader of the senior citizens at Mt. Lebanon and held that role for twelve years. It was my role to organize monthly events for them. What a blessing that became. I was already active as a deacon and growing weekly in praise, worship, and Bible study. But I learned how best to apply that knowledge through the wisdom of these senior souls.

On one of our outings, Mrs. Mary Herman kissed me on the cheek and offered an apology. I asked her for what. When I first moved into the neighborhood, she told her Sunday school class that I would never amount to anything and always be Evil. Her apology still makes me happy when I think of it. She and the others replaced the misery of the back-row life with blessings beyond measure. Change. What a blessing it can be.

Starting over sometimes takes drastic measures. When Tragedy comes, it is easy to be distracted and become angry. Worse yet, it offers a time when we decide to give up on ever being happy or having hope. Don't let that happen to you or someone you love. Surround them with the love that the people at Mt. Lebanon showed us. When loss comes, surround yourself with a church family. The Lord himself plans that resource. Don't overlook it. That humbling fire also had other purposes. Our new home place needed some work. People showed up for the tasks. My father led the work by living with us in a camper behind our mobile home. This fact in itself was a blessing beyond measure. Dad had significantly suffered and responded poorly to the life and death of my mother. But, this mission gave him purpose, and hope returned to him with this project.

The Stewart Home undergoing an upgrade in 1981

What he saw from the family and Mt. Lebanon's support touched his heart. One day, after living in our home for 12 years, he asked me how to be saved. We prayed, and he is now walking the streets of glory. That miracle was unexpected. Dad had I both had our lives changed by efforts from caring Christians. There is always hope for the hopeless—always. Mt. Lebanon is not unique. There is a similar family near you, and it does not have to be a Baptist church. If they claim Christ Jesus as the only way to eternal life and believe he was resurrected from the dead as our savior, give them a chance to become a part of your family.

Some of our weekend friends showed up and offered to replace our lost pot stash with new bags. That offer opened my eyes to what a true friend is. My mother's family included the Gambrell brothers: Stephen, Gerald, David, Danny, Cousins Wayne, and Larry. After the project to up-fit our new home, they stepped forward to expand it. They added three more bedrooms, a larger kitchen, and another bath. Blessings came fast and steady. What the evil agent intended for our destruction, our Lord Jesus turned into an advantage. Those cousins were top-notch and had more than replaced my back-row friends. No one on the Back Row offered to bring hammers and nails. Instead, they offered to provide ways to stay lost.

Changes came fast. My Back Row friends faded into the past, and these new friends entered our lives.

The Gambrell Heroes with Cousins Tony and Becky
Front: Wayne and Stephen Gambrell, Back David and Danny
Gambrell, Tony Stewart, Gerald Gambrell, Becky Edwards McMakin

There was a time when I have pushed away from healthy friends and family members. Thankfully, they did not go away from me. Forgiveness and acceptance are familiar allies to people whose character these people showed me. Fresh starts can come in unexpected ways.

A Change of Friends

The help offered by my weekend party friends burdened me. Mrs. Riley visited simultaneously and testified about relationships with Christian friends that were already heavy on my mind. I also heard from another church member at Mt. Lebanon named Ron Stokes. Ron made it clear that I had a home at his church. He was gentle but persistent. Visits from Elaine Freeman and Yvonne Simpson warmed Kim's heart. Soon, replacements for our weekend friends were lining up to invite us into their families. Our children learned they could spend time with the children at Mt. Lebanon and not watch adults sin on weekends. Second chances abounded. Thank you, Lord.

Still, I was not yet ready to make a complete turnaround. I cautiously moved slowly toward the family of Jesus at Mt. Lebanon Baptist. Stubbornness is a powerful enemy who hates positive change. Out of appreciation for what they did for us, we did make a few visits to attend church there. Early on during this journey, I met the wife of Pastor Delano McMinn. Mrs. Wilene McMinn had a style that eased my fear of the church. Pastor McMinn was also drawing me in with his sermons. But, Sunday morning worship was about as far as I was ready to travel. I had no intentions of joining a Bible study. Mrs. Wilene had a heart for young families. She knew this age group was under attack by the fallen Angel, and she worked hard to invite my age group into the Mt. Lebanon family.

Wilene McMinn worked a different angle on me. She invited me to attend a *"Sausage Biscuit"* class on Sunday mornings at her

home across from the church. That gave Kim a chance to participate in the bible study that Elaine and Yvonne had offered. These
invitations also allowed Anthony and Melanie to join the children's
church. Ron Stokes would also be pleased. So, Bible study began.

Wilene had no other students at first. She was tailoring her
efforts to only me. Soon, others came to test the waters by having
a sausage biscuit breakfast. Wilene, Pastor Delano, Ron, Elaine,
Yvonne, and Georgia Sloan quickly replaced my weekend party
friends. And the number of other healthy church family members grew large also. The conviction was easing up. Blessings were
growing. A change of friends is key to healthy family growth. Just
be careful where you find those friends.

I finally realized that changing the people around me was wise
for our family's future. Since those days, no single book can tell
you of the many blessings that came through that doorway. The
same will be valid for anyone who has chosen friends poorly like
me. These good people knew of my mistakes and loved us in their
homes, church, and trust. I only peeked inside their world. That
was enough for them to rush into mine.

Soon, I learned that Mt. Lebanon had a strong reputation in
sports, especially softball. Before those days, I played softball for
the industrial league teams. So, I approached Pastor McMinn and
proudly offered to join the Mt. Lebanon team. He said that I must
join the church to play and that I needed to be baptized into the
church to become a member.

The baptism in 1983 had more fruit than just joining a soft team.
This act opened many more doors to my growth as a Christian.
What I did as a baptized Christian opened more doors than hitting
a softball ever could. Kim joined the lady's team and played along-
side her mother, Jewel. Years later, Kim, Jewel, and our daughter,
Melanie, played on this team simultaneously. My son Anthony and

I also played on the same team as well. Anthony's and Melanie's children also enjoyed church-related activities.

Blessings beyond measure replaced our competition in the front yard. The word of God replaced a keg of beer.

Today church softball continues to be a gift to all of us and our grandchildren. None of us ever saw these gifts coming. I must also add that Anthony and Melanie have passed Kim and me in skills on the ball field. I suspect the same will become true for our grandchildren. This journey has already begun—no more boxing in the front yard. The changes we made were becoming very good for our family.

Our old weekend friends still came around with drugs, alcohol, and bad advice. I heard a small voice say, shake the dust off your feet and push them away. What we did next was challenging. We advised all old friends that they were welcome if they didn't bring drugs, alcohol, or bad conversations. I also informed them we would do a Bible study while they were present. Most never came back. A few did, and today they number in the minority of those still living in our old circle. Many others fell victim to the same trouble traps I stepped into on the Back Row. Today we still enjoy a precious few of them, including Dave and Renee Robison and Debbie and Steve Rhodes, who are now eternal friends.

I should also offer that our softball teams prospered and won victories on more than just the ball field. Could the reason be that Kim's women's team and my men's team were all in the same Bible study classes? Not one teammate on the men's or women's team at Mt. Lebanon ended up like most of my friends on the Back Row. In addition, Anthony now coaches Mt. Lebanon's men's church team, and Melanie also has a long history of coaching high school at Blue Ridge High. Life coaches come in all varieties. For our family, sports have opened many healthy doorways. There have been many sports trophies that illustrate the quality of sports at

Mt. Lebanon. However, the best treasures from this teamwork are in heaven. You will also find that churches have things for all types of interests, not just sports.

On the map of Good and Evil places I encountered during these years, I saw that I had made my own home a place where Evil grew. I strongly advise against frequenting places of evil. However, Mrs. Riley and many others still chose to visit this Evil place. The difference was that they came, protected by the armor of God. The result was that I am now an eternal child of the risen King Jesus (Eph. 6:10–18).

Fresh starts come in many forms and wear many faces.

Sacrifices

Is making sacrifices required to be a Christian? No. We cannot work our way into heaven. Being saved eternally is a gift. Some tools can help us grow more robust; sacrificing worked for me. I made some sacrifices during the early days when I returned to serve our Lord. I prayed for my family and asked the Lord to bless some sacrifices I made in His name. I gave up music entirely. Sacrificing was an Old Testament way of paying for sins. Jesus has already paid for our sins with His death on the cross. I offer sacrifice not as a way to pay for sins but to rid yourself of distractions in your life.

I threw away all my albums. I cut my long hair, changed the type of clothes I wore, and vowed to be and talk more positively. I quit reading fortune cookies and horoscopes and instead turned to the Bible for answers. There were many more changes I vowed to make. Any sacrifice to honor our Lord strengthens us and makes Jesus smile. I looked at what God had given me and desired to make sacrifices to honor my Saviour.

The smiles of Melanie, Kim & Anthony Stewart
in 1981 influenced my character change.

However, there were a few things that I still hung onto, including pot, beer, and a few pills. In 1983, conviction and a desire to sacrifice joined forces, and I quit all those bad habits cold turkey. The first year was very hard. I still wanted those old enemies. Eventually, cravings for evil things were replaced with surprise gifts. Those gifts were my wife and children. I began to love and appreciate them more. If I started today to write about the blessings they bring to our family, it would be impossible to finish the book. Now that we have Jewel, Zoie, and Emma as grandchildren, the impossibility of recording all they are has grown. It was my family that I leaned on to be drug and alcohol–free since 1983. That victory began thirty-nine years ago.

Surprisingly some sacrifices are given back to us. While I could not and would not grow my hair long again, music returned. Twenty-five years after I gave it up, Mt. Lebanon brought the famous Christian singer Ivan Parker to do a concert in our church. His songs inspired me, especially one called "It's True." This song spoke of a dying father and touched me deeply. For weeks after his concert, I had this song in my head. While in the shower one day, a small voice said, start singing that song now. It had been many years since I sang out loud, but the voice persisted, and I sang out. I could not get that song out of my head. So, I prayed to ask the Lord what He wanted me to do. I heard no answer. Then at one Sunday morning worship service led by our minister of music, Ted Conwell, I listened to the solution. It said, tell Pastor Ted you want to sing. I challenged this voice. Then, Pastor Ted's songs kept saying the same thing to me for several weeks. Ted Conwell is a master of music. His talent can be intimidating, But I had to approach him anyway. I asked Ted if I could sing. He laughingly responded that he did not know I could sing and said I had to audition. I nervously agreed.

That same voice said, "Sing the Ivan Paker song, 'It's True.'" I did, and Ted approved me to sing a solo in our congregation of over 325 people. My voice was back and better than ever. In my haste to return to music, I rushed to buy a Martin acoustic guitar, thinking I could pick a guitar as I did in my rock and roll days. I could not. In my rush to get ahead of our Lord, I assumed He had given me the guitar back. Maybe it will return, but currently, my voice is the only sacrificed item to be returned, and it is not for use in Rock n Roll this time. I have had great joy using that reborn gift. Pastor Ted was the catalyst that returned this gift to me. Find someone in your life like this good man. You will likely find that old gifts can be reborn and new ones taught to grow.

I often see people suffering as I did and can spot a potential future as blessed as mine. When I see someone who has lost their Hope, Peace, or Joy, I see myself and want to point them down the roads I finally followed.

Find a few things to offer our Lord. Such a sacrifice is not required. But, in my case, I found blessings far more significant than anything I gave up. Even if something you sacrifice appears not harmful, you may find that you will see a reward anyway—just a thought. I know a few people that gave up on reading fortune cookies. I know this simple sacrifice can be blessed, as we should only have faith in our future through our Lord Jesus. Small sacrificial offerings can significantly impact your life—even ones of an entertaining type like music, fortune cookies, and horoscopes.

Drug Dealer Becomes
a Police Officer

nlikely outcomes can be expected when you are a child of the risen King Jesus. You can't appreciate that fact if you live in a world that requires proof of everything. Science and logic have a place in our lives. My fifty-plus years in the field of electronics are one example. But to find salvation takes faith first; then, you will see plenty of proof. I consult nationwide with the wealthy and famous on their security and smart house systems. I know logic and the science of technology. This journey to understanding started with the purchase of an Apple computer. I count on science and technology in my profession. However, sadly, some rely solely on evidence and struggle with trusting faith. For the rest of my true story, weigh the events against logic. You will find too many impossible things becoming possible to deny that faith can provide answers that science cannot.

In 1991, in our hometown newspaper, *The Greer Citizen*, I read that the Greer Police Department advertised for reserve police officers. I remembered what the judge said to Attorney Jack Lynn and me seventeen years earlier about me one day being able to be a police officer with a clear criminal record. I applied and was accepted. For twelve weeks, I went to police academy training in the evenings. I passed all tests, and in 1991, I became a Police Officer. This unlikely and seemingly impossible event happened. My wife Kim, Aunt Audrey Stewart Rector, and Father Harry Stewart were at the ceremony. That day was a happy day for them and me. However, that day was also an impossibility that became possible. Logic was replaced with a miracle. In the lives of Christians, noticing miracles is more common than in the logical world.

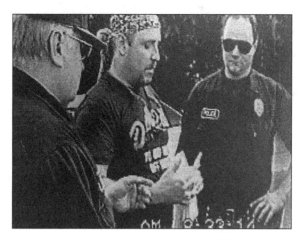

Lt. Steve Selby, Detective Chuck Medford, Officer Tony Stewart

Chief Dean Crisp knew of my drug history and the back-row culture in Greer and asked me to join his narcotics team immediately. Before Chief Crisp's time, some streets in Greer, SC, saw drug deals as an everyday practice. Almost any stranger could drive up and quickly make a buy of crack cocaine. Chief Crisp sent word to the streets that this would end. When I joined them, the team was well along on his campaign. One of the chief's goals was to help the team understand those dealers and predict and counter their new tactics. Small-time dealers continued to sell from street corners. I was to help with this goal. Another goal for me was to work with informants to make buys from the street-corner dealers. While I was eager to help, things had changed since my days on the Back Row. It would take a lot of research to analyze the tactics of the crack cocaine trade. The plan to out-think these dealers was already in place. I only added more human resources. I joined Narcotics Detective Chuck Medford more as free labor than my expertise. The first objective was to claim back the remaining street corners where drug purchases were commonly made.

The chief asked that I not go out in uniform yet, which would blow my cover. However, I could not wait, and the Friday night after I was sworn in, I rode with Sergeant Jimmy Guthrie on patrol and in uniform. Around midnight, our cruiser rolled up on two men taking a leak in the middle of an intersection. Sergeant Guthrie looked into the back of their pickup truck and found a lot of lawn maintenance equipment. He asked if they could produce proof of purchase. They could not but said an uncle could. Sgt. Guthrie asked to have him come to the police station with those receipts and allowed the men to follow us there. I spent over an hour in front of those men while we waited. I was in full uniform. The uncle came and proved ownership, and the men were let go with only a gentle scolding from Sgt. Guthrie. Such was his nature. Jimmy was a big, powerful man. I never saw him use his size to solve problems. My first lesson as a police officer was using conversation to solve issues and show mercy to offenders.

Sergeant Jimmy Guthrie

I saw my pending role as a Police Officer as a way that I could pay back some old dues. I should have known that paying any dues was not spiritually sound and that the Lord Jesus had other plans for my time in this uniform. Getting started with Jimmy Guthrie taught me many things I would need later. Patience and compassion was my first lesson. While I pushed past the requests of Chief Crisp to not wear a uniform yet, the Lord used my disobedience to teach me some valuable lessons.

The following weekend, I took off my uniform, got into a loaned personal vehicle with an informant, and went to a street corner, hoping to make my first crack cocaine buy. To my surprise, standing on that very first corner was one of the two men I spent time with when I was in uniform just days before. I just knew I *"was burned."* But, I asked him if he had anything to sell me. The man standing with him advised that he did not know me and did not want to sell to me. However, the man that should know me as a cop reported to his friend that he did know me and that it would be OK to sell to me. It would be easy to comment about how stupid this man was. But, the compassionate lesson that Jimmy Guthrie had taught me overcame my desire to criticize, and instead, I became burdened for him. We would make many more buys on this street corner and others before my drug-buying time ended, and the "roundup" of all the street dealers happened. Each deal touched my heart. I saw no joy when these people sold to me. Instead, I prayed for them and their families.

I felt that my first buy was a fluke, but I met numerous drug dealers who acted similar to the first over the next few years. The drug of choice had changed from my days as a drug dealer on the Back Row, but paying attention had not improved. I bought from one dealer nine different times. Later, when we made the round-up arrests of all the dealers who sold to me, I was in uniform. I arrested this dealer who had seen me nine times before as a buyer. He became irritated and claimed he had not sold to an undercover agent. He swore that if I could put this officer in front of him, he would tell him to his face that he was a liar. He was looking at the officer when he said that. My heart grew heavier. No joy came when I put handcuffs on him or others who sold to me.

I made dozens of buys from dozens of dealers. When the court date came, Greer Narcotics Detective Chuck Medford and I wore a suit and ties and waited for each trial to begin. While standing against a courthouse wall, one of the lawyers I knew from my drug-dealer court dates walked by and recognized me. He asked why I was there. I said for a drug trial. He chewed me out and stated that he remembered me getting a conditional discharge and that he had never seen this sentence before or since. He complained that I had learned nothing. I smiled. He chewed me out for smiling, but I said something was different. He chewed me out again, stating that nothing was different. I pulled my suit coat back to show him my badge on my belt. He questioned its authenticity. Detective Medford assured him it was real and that the docket's cases that day were from buys I had made. Impossible outcomes do happen. I am proof. While getting a criminal record cleaned is rare with a *"Conditional Discharge"* sentence, miracles are not. You must have faith they can happen to you. My first role as a police officer was a sign that anything is possible if the Lord is your Savior. That act had the hand of God on it. Proof does not exist of that fact, that is, unless you believe in miracles.

There certainly is hope for the hopeless. But what about the souls who sold the drugs to me? They, too, might feel hopeless. I lost track of some of them, but others stayed on similar roads of trouble throughout their lives. Many of these men spent no time incarcerated or received only short sentences. One of them I saw again soon. Detective Medford and I began to patrol the streets together after those trials. One night we rolled up on a lady friend of one of those dealers. She was bleeding from the mouth badly. Her man did not get jail time and was back on the street, selling again. He had taken a drink from a bottle and slammed it into her mouth to break out her teeth. Why? Because she had used some of the dope she was selling for him. She also had his stash of crack cocaine hidden in their baby's diaper that she was holding. We did not charge her for that. We just disposed of it correctly and called her an ambulance.

She said she would testify against him. So, after the ambulance took her to the hospital, we looked for him and found him and another dealer on the street corner nearby. We asked why he did that to his lady during a field interview. His response was to throw punches at us and then run away. We chased him down and arrested him. His lady dropped her charges against him. At his trial for throwing punches at us, we were not allowed to tell of her injuries because she chose not to testify against him. The jury decided we had no business interviewing him on the street corner, and, He was judged innocent.

That night, the youth pastor from Mt. Lebanon Baptist rode with us as an observer. That night changed his heart forever. Like most of us cops, he saw the horrible crimes and developed a burden for those living in this sin. Police officers are not allowed to tell of the hidden horrors they encounter. Instead, they can only let that Evil burn inside their souls. Police Officers know of great need but must walk cautiously around those burdens.

The People We Meet While in Police Uniform

F ar too many calls for the services of a police officer resulted in officers being asked to be more than arresting agents. We were often asked to listen to the problems of those we met and give advice. I often left a trouble call with a burden for the victim and the criminal. The same was true for all the officers I worked alongside. Sadly, we all felt that our hands were tied, could often only listen, and were not allowed to counsel. We all saw violent tragedies and deaths. Compassion existed but had to stay hidden. Please make no mistake about it. Police officers are not tough guys by choice. We must wear that face as part of our jobs. The depth of loss that we see weighs heavily on all of us. We hoped for rescues for those we served, and some of us prayed for this. But, sadness always remained as our burden.

I took this burden to the office of our senior pastor at Mt. Lebanon Baptist at the time. Pastor Scott Mcalister was also affected by what I told him. I wanted to be a police officer, but this was not what I expected. I was hurting over these people, and after hearing the stories from our youth pastor and me, he asked our deacons to do a ride-along with us. He also rode along. What they saw impacted them like it did all of us officers.

The chief's goal of reclaiming the street corners was eventually a success. Chief Crisp formed a "jump-out" team who rode through these neighborhoods in private vans and quickly clarified that this kind of public crime would not be permitted. I was on the jump-out squad but was in uniform this time. Each arrest that came did not heal my hurting heart. The same was true for most of the other officers. There were no celebrations of joy. These good men just did what was needed and went home with burdens. I never heard any racial comments at all. Instead, I listened to expressions of sorrow over the lifestyles of these criminals and their victims. At no time did the "jump out" team abuse anyone. Instead, we made our presence known on streets where the word was out that the police would never come. We were all prejudiced against the Evil that ruined so many lives, regardless of the skin color of the victims.

On many occasions, the neighbors in the neighborhoods thanked us. One lady said that after several years of locking her doors in the dark and never going outside until daylight, she finally could walk her street and feel safe. On other occasions, cakes, cookies, and food arrived at the jail.

There are stories of terrible things done by police officers. But the news media tends to major on the minor few. Instead, most law enforcement officials do their jobs because they are called to do so and certainly not for the money. I have served alongside Greenville County Sheriff Hobart Lewis and the current Greer Police Chief Matt Hamby. I also know of the quality of the work by Spartanburg County Sheriff Chuck Wright. These men lead wisely, and those under them work because of a calling, not a paycheck. The same is true for the vast majority of law-enforcement agencies. Let us all be careful not to major on the few minor officers who make horrible mistakes.

Greer SC Chief Matt Hamby, Greenville County Sheriff Hobart
Lewis, Spartanburg County Sheriff Chuck Wright

The Evil One himself is the hidden source of the move to
defund the police. This nemesis of order wants to destroy the
calling to serve the public as a law officer. That is the hidden goal
of the enemy, nothing else. Sadly, some bad officers' horrible acts
are all you hear about on the news. Yes, let us punish this. But let
us also promote the excellent officers as heroes. They are the vast
majority, and they seldom make the news.

Try to picture a future world Satan would design. It would be
one without law and order. Instead of defunding, let's provide pay
raises. On the other hand, these same street corner criminals were
people like I once was. Each had a loss that placed them where
they were.

On December 5, 1976, at the Greer Memorial Hospital, I was
waiting on the birth of my son Anthony and thinking back to
my arrest for drug trafficking on the Back Row. The Greer officer
who had made that arrest arrived and sat beside me to await the
birth of his daughter. This man was one of two of the same officers who carried me to jail in the back of a pickup truck. We spoke,
and I learned he had the same feelings I am describing now. He
had no joy when arresting me. From that day forward, I realized
that law enforcement officers have compassion and that their duty

sometimes hurts. There is no joy in incarcerating most people. The chance meeting with this officer stuck with me and helped me decide to serve as a Police Officer one day.

That desire began in 1991 when I, too, became a Greer Police Officer and grew as I met others calling for help who, like me, had been defeated. If you plan to make noise about how bad the police are, do this first: find a local agency that will let you ride along. One night should change your mind. Before you criticize, take a look from the other side.

Occasionally, I was able to arrest someone who was hurting others. Crack cocaine dealers qualified, but I could not harden my heart against them. For each arrest, there was little joy. What Pastor Scott learned from his ride-along fueled his passion. The church he soon started is always ready to help the hurting. The name of that church is Springwell Church in Taylors, SC.

Once I became a police officer, it became essential to study the tactics used by street-corner drug dealers. We would use dark clothes to better blend into the dark shadows of the evil streets we snuck through. Our goal was to get as close to the dealers who sold on the street corners as possible. Detective Medford and I would discreetly enter the areas of concern, watch, and listen. We could often get so close to the dealers that we could hear every word that spoke. We also watched their actions when a spotter shouted that a police car on patrol was approaching. Often they would quickly stash their supply of drugs nearby. We would then radio the patrol car to stop and pick it up. We often could not make an arrest, but we did take a lot of crack cocaine off the streets. This way, getting crack off the streets was satisfying because no one needed to use handcuffs.

What I did not expect was this the intelligence we gathered often fueled compassion for these criminals. I learned of the life burdens they lived through daily. The same is true for all officers of the law. Making arrests did not accompany a feeling of victory.

Pastor Scott McAlister asked to ride with us again, and we began a time when the three of us would tactfully get close to the dealers, to watch and listen. Pastor Scott heard conversations spoken loudly by dealers that broke his heart like it had mine. He saw men abuse their women and their children. Pastor Scott heard horrible things they had done or planned to do. He learned that the conversations on the street corners were loud, boastful, and damaging. The pastor watched as men would use their women to hold their drugs and saw drugs hidden in their children. He saw what happened when the count of drugs the women or even young children sold did not meet their expectations. Pastor Scott saw Evil that he could not believe existed.

Pastor Scott McAlister

Afterward, Detective Medford and I openly rode around these neighborhoods in unmarked cars. We would stop and talk with many of these people. The main drug dealers would not speak with us. But, many everyday people would. Plenty of good people live in bad situations and neighborhoods. My wife Kim learned this while riding with us one night. That sweltering summer night, we stopped near a group of children walking the streets at 2 a.m. We asked them their ages and why they were outside without an adult. Their ages ranged from five to ten. They had searched trash cans for something to eat, and one of them had some slices of partially eaten pizza. Detective Medford and I knew their parents and that being outside those homes was better than being inside—a sad fact that we knew from being inside their homes. This kind of lifestyle forever touched Kim. Law officers are not babysitters but are often expected to be so. However, they are often restricted by poorly written laws.

Those who have been in law enforcement understand this kind of lifestyle. In my fourteen years as a cop, I never heard anyone talk critically about the hopelessness we encountered. Instead, we lived with these people's burdens on our hearts. We just shook it off and went on to the next call. We became numb by realizing that these children had limited chances for a good start in their lives. This lifestyle is still common today. These burdens are precisely who the Lord Jesus walked this earth to reach. They are people just like we are. They are His children, and they are loved. Cops can't walk away from their crimes, but they walk away with their burdens. Children of poor parenting become Generationally Cursed themselves. Jesus can break that curse as he did for me. Police Officers best not offer that advice.

Early in my police career, I knew I would not write traffic tickets. I would undoubtedly make arrests, but I desired to be merciful. I only wrote one traffic ticket in my fourteen years because Chief

Crisp was with me, but I tore it up later. Sorry, Chief. In this small way, I could help others who, like me, had lived a life similar to my back-row experiences. In this small way, I could help the hopeless.

Thank the Lord Jesus for Christians who are open to being the doorway for others to find second chances and fresh starts.

Springwell Church, 4369 Wade Hampton Blvd, Taylors, SC, 29687

Lessons Learned

mainly worked on weekends and chose to work during the late-night power shifts. Reserve officers had the flexibility to select which officer would be our partner. Chief Crisp allowed Reserves to check out a cruiser and work alone. I decided not to work alone and only drove a patrol car alone to get through that part of my mandatory training.

Pastor Scott sent deacons to ride with my partner and me on weekends. Deacon David Farnham rode with us and spent his time finding ways to extend a helping hand to everyone we encountered. He was next on the list of those our Lord sent to teach me. The Lord Jesus had already gone above and beyond to put me in this role. I knew that I was not here only to arrest people. Instead, it was to be a ministry for Him. However, there is such a thing as separation of church and state. David Farnham taught me how to navigate this handicap without violating man's law while answering calls for help wisely.

I watched as people we encountered and even other officers were attracted to Him before David opened his mouth to speak. Today I am reminded of the attraction people must have had to Jesus when I think of David Farnham. He also found a way not to mix church and state. The way he did so was to wait until someone asked where they could find help. He would gently and legally lead them to answer that question themselves. They were always the ones who spoke the name of Jesus or his church first. After this lesson, I learned to offer help when asked and only when the people I encountered brought up the subject of Jesus first. The character of David Farnham is present in many officers, but the danger of sharing Jesus restricts them.

The evil named Fear was often present when we responded to calls for help. I learned that Peace was an excellent tool to use against fear. Before starting a shift at the police department, I did not pray for my safety. Instead, I prayed that I could be used to deliver peace as a counter to fear. This prayer was answered many times. I knew that I had to balance the separation of church and state. David had taught me how to do that.

I often chose to ride with some officers who had struggles themselves. I found in them a common desire to help others. They, like I, had lived alongside Evil and now had a heart for the lost and struggling people they encountered. Mercy was shared whenever possible. You may find it uncommon that law officers care so much about the victims they face. This thought is under attack by the fallen Angel. He is busy at work to make the image of Peace Officers change to one of Evil. He is a liar. Peace Officer is still the correct description for these men and women.

If I can share any lesson in this story, let it be that the Peace Officer stands on the front lines of the battle against evil. They stand ready to offer second chances. The news media don't cover that goal of their job.

Visit From an Angel on New Years' Eve

There were times when I saw peaceful evenings. But there were also times when Evil reigned. Some nights, his presence was so strong that I could almost smell his breath. There were also plenty of times when he boasted openly about his trophies. Fear was always a factor in his goal to hurt. I saw Death claim its victims in many different ways. Pain, Infidelity, Drunkenness, Addiction, and many other Fallen Angel agents saw no need to hide. The map I could make of places where evil had set up a residence was already large and growing.

On occasion, when I made an arrest, and right after I handcuffed a person, Evil would speak through him and attack me as a Chrisitan. Such things happened to other Christian officers as well. The forces that police officers have to deal with include more than just Evil in people. The enemy, Satan, feels that he does not need to hide at these crossroads. Amid such evil domains, he gloats and speaks out loud. The good news exists that the angel agents of our Lord also often talk to us in human form.

Our police chaplain was Pastor Keith Kelly of His Vineyard Church. Pastor Keith was the mentor to many officers and the troubled souls we encountered. Men like him put their lives on the line to stand ready to help the hurting. Chaplains see these forces of evil appear often. While I was not a Chaplain, Pastor Keith, Pastor Scott, and Deacon David were championing against the Evil officer's encounter. Their help was greatly appreciated. These men often stepped into harm's way alongside officers. And they had no protection except the armor of God.

His Vineyard 656 Arlington Road, Greer SC, 29651

I was punched, slapped, bit, and spit on many times. I was attacked with boards and knives and had guns pointed at me. I even had my foot stomped several times. Being cursed became common. The evil named Violence shows itself to our officers frequently. They get paid but not enough for what they do. Reserve officers like me did not get paid at all.

My days of violent reactions to situations had ended before becoming a Peace Officer. I did not return attacks against me with violent responses. Instead, I had Peace inside me that ruled my reactions. The same was true for my fellow officers. That's why we were called Peace Officers.

One frigid NewYears' eve, I rode with my partner, Travis Stamey. Travis and I complemented each other's styles and shared a lot of near-death events. The night before, I had an intense dream of Travis and me both getting shot while stopped at an intersection. In that dream, both of us were killed. That dream was very vivid and worrisome. The Lord has used dreams to share visions with me before, and each time, the things shared proved to be a warning of an actual event.

Officer Travis Stamey

Early that evening, Travis and I patrolled a closed car lot. There we found Pastor Keith Kelly looking at cars. We talked, and he advised that he had recently had a vision related to our safety. We ended our talk with prayer. His vision would soon prove accurate, and His intercessory prayer would be answered.

After midnight, we stopped at a convenience store to get some coffee. There was a stranger there who asked for a ride home. He had no coat, was dressed oddly, and wore a long beard like Jesus. He wanted to go a long way outside the city limits, and we requested permission from the duty sergeant to go out of our jurisdiction to take him there. Usually, the answer would be no because it would take us away from patrol, and that night, we were short-staffed anyway. The sergeant radioed back, asking if Preacher Stewart was making the request? That was the first time I would be called preacher; it would not be the last. He permitted us.

We began the trip and asked our guest his name. He answered just as we passed a roadside cross with the name of an infant named Charles on it. This infant had recently died at that intersection in a car wreck. Our passenger hesitated and said his name was Charles. He then spoke to us about tragedies at crossroads and resulting deaths. His conversation was intense—our patrol car filled with a feeling of peace.

During the trip, the dispatcher radioed about shots being fired at an intersection back in the city limits. All of our officers were busy and could not respond. We were too far away and had Charles as a passenger. When we turned into the driveway, he thanked us, warned us of danger at our crossroads, and got out of our cruiser. Travis asked where he went, wanting to watch him enter the home at the end of this long driveway? We both looked for him, and he was gone. *Completely gone!* The driveway was over 300 feet long, with an open field on both sides. He just disappeared.

When we returned to the City, we drove past where the shots were overhead to be fired. The person making the calls advised that he was shouting that he wanted to kill someone and shouted that if the cops came, he would kill them. The vision in my dream matched the area exactly. Charles was an Angel from heaven, believe it or not. This time Charles the Angel used distraction against the plan of the Fallen One to kill us both. Our Lord Jesus's forces can always counter evils like Distractions. This tactic is standard in the Spiritual Warfare Battlefield. This night, Travis and I received rescues.

Other times, Evil was out in the open, and Angels of Good battled them. I never saw those battles, but I know they existed. Sadly, Evil claimed too many victories, and the map of places where evil chose to flex his muscles grew. There were times when I could feel the presence of Evil surround us. Those were times when Pastors and Deacons provided a much-needed prayer cover.

On that journey with Charles, Travis and I both received Second Chances.

My Last Day as a Police Officer

R eserve officers like myself could choose when we worked and who we rode with occasionally. I often chose Corporal Paul. One evening in 2005, while on patrol with him, we observed an oncoming vehicle with a headlight flickering on and off. Corporal Paul turned around and caught up with the car while I ran the license plate on our mobile unit. The license plate did not match the model and brand of the car it was on. While the flickering headlight might not have resulted in a traffic stop, we could not overlook the improper license plate.

My partners knew that mercy would be another companion with us when I was their partner. Most of the partners I rode with had a similar disposition. Often there are several ways to handle a traffic stop. A safety warning for the headlight was possible as long as no other major violation was present. Corporal Paul knew I would ask for mercy and was willing to provide the same.

We turned on our blue lights, and the driver pulled over in the Second Baptist Church parking lot on Memorial Drive Extension. While on duty, I often experienced spiritual warfare. This night would be no exception. Even the location of this traffic stop had the handprint of our Lord. Sacred grounds like the home of Second Baptist church always have Guardian Angels assigned to them. That night, they stood ready immediately after we entered the parking lot. I did not know if this would be my last day as a Police Officer or if that place would become a battlefield. A new battle was waging, but our Lord had placed its beginning on one of his sacred grounds.

Corporal Paul approached the driver's side, and I, the passenger. My role was to keep the passenger side safe while Corporal Paul communicated with the driver. It was a noisy road, and I could not hear Corporal Paul's words to the driver. Instead, he signaled me that an arrest was likely. My role then became communicating with and keeping the passenger calm until Corporal Paul could advise me of the driver's disposition.

I suspected the improper license plate was not the reason for the pending arrest. Something beyond was likely the cause of the arrest. Over my fourteen years of service, I realized that officers had no driving desire to arrest. My time of service saw interactions with Greenville and Spartanburg County Deputies and Duncan, Lyman, Inman, Simpsonville, Mauldin, and Wellford City officers. They all shared the same character trait of being merciful when possible. Adding another burden onto people who already had a heavy load was not the goal. These officers had developed the ability to listen more to people than give orders for them to follow. The result was that the souls we encountered usually stayed peaceful. There were times when this did not happen, but there were more opportunities to show mercy than to arrest in most encounters.

Being merciful and gentile was my goal on that hot summer night's traffic stopped. It began when I asked this lady who she was and learned that the driver was her husband. She stayed calm for the moment. Corporal Paul advised that the driver had a suspended license. In addition, the car had no insurance. Driving under suspension is a violation where an arrest is typical. Allowing the vehicle to be moved is also not possible until insurance covers it. As gently as I could, I told this lady that her husband had to go to jail for driving under suspension. The uninsured car could not be driven away without insurance and would be towed to a storage lot by their choice of wrecker services. When learning of this, she became irate.

There are often several ways to handle an arrest. Writing tickets was not always required. My desire to promote hope through mercy often impacted the City of Greer's revenue. However, I had never heard such a conversation from our leadership. Meeting such a quota is not a standard requirement. Instead, the welfare and health of our citizens were more of a concern of upper management. I can also attest that the other local agencies around Greer, SC had a similar disposition. Cops are not your enemies. Chief Dean Crisp taught the other officers and me many such principles.

Just before the night of this traffic stop, Chief Crisp had left the Greer PD and taken the job as the Chief of Police in Columbia, SC. The value system he embedded into his officers continued. How we handled, this traffic stop would be no exception.

Before we transported this gentleman to jail, I advised the lady I would ask my partner if he could do anything to show mercy. She then calmed down a little and changed her show of anger to one of concern. She asked about towing the car and stated that they had made the drive to get some needed groceries. Now, I shared her burden. I had been at similar crossroads in my own life and knew what it was like to suffer while trying to navigate through troubled roads. I had not spoken to Corporal Paul yet, but he knew what I would be asking. We talked, and he agreed to let this man sign his bond and reduce the ticket cost. As policy required, He handcuffed the man and placed him in the back seat while waiting on the wrecker. Before I could tell her of the mercy Corporal Paul was to show, she lost her peace again, and anger ruled once again. We talked slowly, and she calmed a little when she heard Corporal Paul's offer of mercy.

She asked if she could drive the car home. I advised that proof of insurance was required before the vehicle could be on the road again. She pointed to the groceries on the back seat and mentioned that the meat and ice cream would ruin. My goal as a police officer always included being at the crossroads of people that needed mercy. I had to do something to prevent or reduce the loss of food. We asked if they had a wrecker company of choice and anyone who could come to get the groceries before the wrecker arrived. They answered no to both questions. She lost control again. Insults toward us followed. Sometimes, too many times, this is the response to such situations. Officers tire of being insulted when they are only enforcing the law. After an intense verbal attack, it's less likely that mercy will follow. But in this case, Officer Paul and I still had compassion.

Mercy is quite often the first choice with police officers. However, some violations do not qualify for mercy. This time mercy in the form of reduced costs, and a release on his word, was available and was given. To prevent the loss of spoiled food, I reached into my wallet and pulled out $40, all the cash I had on me, and gave it to her to replace her spoiled groceries. If I had more, I would have given it all. I often witnessed other officers do the same. The critical point is that mercy is more common in law enforcement than the media writes.

While waiting on the wrecker to arrive, I had more time to talk with this lady. She shared how their luck had recently been insufficient and how they had reached out to local agencies and resources only to find little help. This lifestyle is the definition of hopeless. Hopelessness is why I wanted to be a police officer. I felt that my experiences of despair and the peace I later found was reason to stand ready to help others. I found hope when I was more desperate than anyone I encountered as a police officer. Who better to understand the burdens of others than I? Providing even a little hope was always my goal while in police uniform.

She specifically asked me where they could find hope. She wondered where she could turn. I mentioned a study session I held once a week for people like her who were in hard times and asked to mail her an invitation. She said yes and provided an address. During our time together, I never mentioned the name of Jesus Christ. Instead, I spoke of a class I taught on how to find hope again. I often said that I was a convicted drug dealer who had a clean record and was even able to become a police officer. I spoke of the events that had robbed me of hope. I told of people who stood at my crossroads, ready to guide me down healthy pathways wisely. I said of the times I pushed away those offers of help only to continue on my path of hopelessness. In such talks, the emphasis is that some healthy life coaches only appear once. She and I spoke that spotting these life coaches is vital. She agreed and asked for more examples. She had finally become calm again. She had heard of a road to hope that intrigued her.

I asked her if I could mail her a letter with more details about this pathway to hope. She was eager to provide an address. I asked for an address that was not on their driver's license. I advised that I wanted to keep that information private to separate my letter from my duties as a Police Officer. She provided such an address. I closed this conversation by stating that my letter would be blunt and to the point. It would include that our chance encounter could be a one-time crossroads event. She agreed. I did not mention that this class was a part of a bible study. I also never said the name of Jesus. Instead, I promoted that hope was the result of this class. Christianity or a related discussion was never a part of my interactions while in a police uniform. When the letter arrived, she would learn of my desire to represent Christ.

While waiting on a wrecker to arrive, she spoke of her Doctorate in Religion. She interestingly told of Druidism, of which I knew very little. I found this lady to be very articulate and educated. In my talks with this lady, there was no mention of religion. Instead, I only replied to her, asking where they could go to find hope. Even the location of the class was not inside our church.

In these classes, Jesus was the core of the message. However, on the streets of Greer and in my police uniform, I did not open up a single conversation about Jesus. Instead, I mailed invitations. I felt good about how we handled this traffic stop and left that night, hoping I would see her at an upcoming Sunday morning class.

I prayed not for my safety for the fourteen years of my service. Instead, I prayed to be a life coach at the crossroads of someone who lost hope as I had myself. There were many answered prayers. To ensure my prayers were righteous, I had to be sure not to violate man's laws. I could not and did not preach while on duty. From my own home and not while on duty, I did send letters that explained how I had found hope. This lady did receive a letter. I never meant for it to insult her. Knowing that I had one chance to reach her, I did intend for it to make a definite impact. I closed our talks by saying that my letter would be direct. I asked her forgiveness for the blunt words that would follow in my invitation letter. She agreed. My words had worked well before. In this example, things did not go as they had previously.

That letter could have opened the door to fresh starts that she said they needed.

How I Met the ACLU

I mailed her the invitation the next day. The invitation mentioned that the Lord Jesus sends help, but a response is required to provide guidance. This invitation also advised that no answer to the Lord's offer of help invites more Evil into our lives. I was specific and blunt with this truth. It was in response to her question about where they could find help. My Lord would hold me accountable if I did anything less in my response to her questions.

A few days later, I was in my office at our family business, Stewart Electronics, when our secretary advised that a news reporter from one of the largest national news agencies was on the line wanting to interview me. I picked up the phone and asked the lady about the reason for the interview? She wondered if her agency could be the first to question the Baptist preacher who handcuffed a Druid princess on the side of the road and preached to her while in police uniform? I made no reply and ended the call. In minutes the TV trucks from three of the four local TV channels arrived in our parking lot with their TV cameras and asked the exact interview requests. I heard the lady's name from the traffic stop mentioned by them all. No interviews by the Police Department of myself or Corporal Paul had yet happened. The news media published what they wanted without asking us for the truth. This lady was never arrested and indeed never handcuffed. She was not made to listen to preaching but mailed a letter instead. The news media did not tell of the mercy shown to her husband and the $40 I gave her. These facts never made it to the media, or if they did, they chose not to share them.

This incomplete and errant news quickly grew through worldwide news sources. I got an email from a friend traveling in Europe asking about this. He had heard the same stories on a local TV channel. At this early stage, the search for truth was not a priority. Possibly fueled by my lack of willingness to provide an interview, distortions, lies, and deceit grew. I was left to believe that a driving force with most, not all, news media sources is to sell stories, even without proof of accuracy. The lady and her husband did interviews. They promoted that I did not separate church from state. Later, the Greer Police Department did an internal investigation. The results were that Corporal Paul and I did not violate their policy of separating church from state. This ruling made very little news. Most did not carry it.

In the early days, I learned that the ACLU was involved and had approached the press before they approached our police department. It is likely that they, too, heard the unproven story from the news media. Things began to take some unhealthy twists after this. The lady let our new police chief read the invitation letter. And he also shared it with the media, adding his opinion that something was wrong. He had not yet spoken to me to get the truth. Soon, the press was roasting me again. The new police Chief in Greer had rushed to judgment. The ACLU and the media took that as an open door to attack. Truth fell victim to Evil that day, temporarily. Many variations of the untruth circulated before the City of Greer ruled I did not act unlawfully. For several months, I stayed silent. But, our Lord was preparing to use this entire event to his advantage. I saw and continue to see more than I lost on that journey.

Today, the web still has stories of untruths. None that I have seen tell the entire story truthfully. Reports circulated that we pulled them over because they had a bumper sticker stating "It's a Druid Thing" and that I was a Baptist minister and used that as the reason to pull the car over. I was not a Baptist minister. The bumper sticker played no role in the traffic stop. When the police department conducted the internal investigation, they listened to the radio traffic that led up to the traffic stop. They heard that the faulty headlight began the event. They listened to no mention of a bumper sticker. Instead, they saw that the improper license plate was the reason for the stop.

Much of what the press told of was their interpretation (or lack thereof). That night, bad luck fell on that couple. The news media added to the misery with their willingness to propagate rather than investigate. Not all media sources distort stories. One of the local TV stations chose not to spread this news. Another source of credible reporting was our hometown newspaper, the Greer Citizen. The Burch family owned this new source and traditionally focused on truth first. Due to this family's depth of Christian character, the City of Greer saw wholesome reporting for several generations. Their positive influence helped my local support group grow. The Burch family also operated a radio station where I once worked as an apprentice disc jockey in the 10th grade. Had it not been for the lessons of integrity I learned from the Burch family, I would have given up on any news source ever speaking the truth long ago. The whole truth is out there, but it is under constant attack. Be careful what you trust as the truth—stories of good sell less often than those of wrong. The Evil army uses some news media resources proudly as an ally.

Had this lady attended the study I invited her to, she would surely have heard the name of Jesus Christ. That meeting would have been the first time she heard me proselytize. These classes were across the road from my home church of Mt. Lebanon Baptist. There was no dress code or pressure to attend the following worship services across the street. People who were searching for hope sat beside others with the same goal. My goal for this class included sharing the resource Mt. Lebanon Baptist had been to me on my journey to healing.

Some of the students did migrate to the worship services and began a life filled with hope, peace, and joy. I preached at the funerals of several of those who attended this class. Some of which I was able to speak words of celebration.

I can not tell you what the goal of the ACLU was during this time. I am aware that they have had a positive impact on other people. In my case, it did not work out that way. I know there was a lot of pressure from somewhere to end my police career. I have often wondered if threats of lawsuits resulted in out-of-court pay-offs or settlements or my dismissal. I may never know. During the early days of this ordeal, the City of Greer dropped the Reserve Police officer program completely, and six of us turned in our uniforms. My days as an unpaid Greer City Police Officer ended.

Corporal Paul also lost his job. An unrelated unlawful arrest that night resulted in his firing, and he signed a document stating that he would never be a police officer anywhere else. The City of Greer also gave the ACLU a written letter that I would never be allowed to be a police officer for them again. Corporal Paul's supposed unlawful arrest occurred later that night when he and I came across a home with a raging brush fire in the backyard with nobody monitoring it. We stopped to ask the resident to go outside and take care of it. They must not have looked out to see who was knocking. When they opened the back door, I spotted an open suitcase with almost a pound full of marijuana on the floor just inside the door. It was evident that they were selling those drugs and were ready to sell more when we knocked. Corporal Paul and the shift sergeant on duty made those arrests. However, there was a problem. That house was one house outside Greer City Limits. Their charges were dropped, and they were released.

The timing of these events was suspicious to me and others. We all wondered if the ACLU had made demands for the dismissal of Corporal Paul related to the traffic stop. I can only say that Evil ruled that night, and we both lost our badges. The ACLU did threaten lawsuits, or at least the media thought so. When this news spread, some formidable allies stepped forward to defend me. Corporal Paul had no role in my actions with the lady that night. So, he did not see any supporters of his cause. Sadly, Greer lost an excellent cop that night. Corporal Paul was that officer.

A Spartanburg First Baptist Church representative, Mr. William Renfrow, visited my Pastor Mark Smith and me, offering to provide all funds for any legal defense I might need. Their church was also the home church of Pastor Billy Graham. Their prayer cover alone would have been enough, but they stepped forward to battle the ACLU as needed. I also received a visit from Mr. Ken Howard as a representative from Praise Cathedral in Greer. They also offered to provide attorneys to defend me and provide prayer cover. They were another church in a long list of those providing support. The prayer cover alone won many unseen battles during those days. Our Lord Jesus had another plan for my future that would show much more ground gained than was ever lost. These churches and others like them were ready to defend the right to speak the name of Jesus.

Pastor Mark Smith also fielded phone calls of support from other nationally known support sources. He even took calls from members of the witchcraft community. One of them identified herself as a White-Witch, advising that other evil witches would be attacking Mt. Lebanon Baptist Church and me. After the Greer Police Department cleared me of any wrongdoing, Local Attorneys approached me related to a defamation lawsuit.

Unless we surround ourselves with a proven list of Christian Life Coaches, it is challenging to see through the clutter and spot our Lord's outstretched hands. However, during this time, healthy Life Coaches surrounded me. I also prayed that the same would be valid for the lady, her husband, and Corporal Paul.

A few weeks later, after the City cleared me of any wrongdoing, I was asked to appear on WGGS's Christian television program *Nightline*. The topic was the separation of church and state. This show lasted several weeks and allowed my gift of song to return. More importantly, it brought forth more prayer warriors who added to the active army that defended me. Witches, Druids, and the ACLU combined would not see victory against these prayer warriors' intercessory work.

My police career had ended, which evolved into invitations to preach and speak at churches. These events signaled the beginning of a vision my Grandmother, LuVadie Gambrell, shared with me many years earlier. During some of my most hopeless days, she saw through the evil and into my future when she told me I would preach one day. I love and miss you, Grandmother. You were right. Save me a seat at the feet of Jesus. What Evil meant for harm can always become a victory. A peace beyond description has replaced my badge. This kind of victory is possible, even for the most hopeless souls.

I believe the lady and her husband played little if any role in this event's direction. She was simply at a crossroads where she needed help. I, too, have been at similar crossroads. The hidden enemy during these days was Satan. He was looking for a way to end my offers of mercy to people I encountered while representing the great City of Greer, SC. For a time, his plan worked. However, this story touched the hearts of many people that I could not have reached while in uniform. The damages that evil planned turned into blessings. Because of that traffic stop and threats against my future, lost lives found hope. What Evil meant for harm, God reversed for good. This resource is always available. Always!

Haste is the name of a powerful enemy of good. We must always be careful to pray through our reactions to crossroads situations. Greer's Chief of Police rushed to comment on the letter I mailed. The media and the ACLU keyed in on his reply, and things snowballed into some harmful directions. Soon, it appeared that things were out of control. They were not. The result was a blessing beyond measure.

In my years in the Air Force, I had an immature desire to help people. I did not know then that helping others was not wise when I was dancing with Evil myself. My desire to assist a friend who had a drug addiction when I had significant problems was not an intelligent recipe for success. The difference between the battle while I was in the USAF and the one while I was a Police Officer was that I had a support group in the latter one. Find, and join a support group. You must not navigate through troubled times by yourself.

Below is a partial list of churches that actively prayed for intervention for me. There were many more not mentioned. I offer these people and each church as havens of hope. There are similar places near each of you. Find and join one. Second chances abound in such sites.

BAPTIST CHURCHES:
Mt. Lebanon, Washington, Apalache, New Jerusalem, Victor, El Bethel, Ebenezer Welcome, Spartanburg First, Greer First, Greer Second, Northwood, Pelhan First, Holly Springs, Fairview, Pleasant Grove, Locust Hill, Friendship, Taylors First, Double Springs, Mayfield Chapel, Duncan First, Blue Ridge, Highlands, Pleasant Hill, and many more.

UNITED METHODIST CHURCHES:
Victor, Memorial, Grace, Fews Chapel, and many more.

CHURCH OF GOD:
Praise Cathedral, Woodruff, and many more.

NON-DENOMINATIONAL:
Grace Church, Rushing Wind, His Vineyard, Springwell, Carolina Faith Riders.

The Back Row Becomes a City Park

W hile on the *Nightline* TV show, I made several mistakes that I must apologize for now. My words led others to believe that our city leaders were something they were not. There were so many threats in front of me that I made assumptions without facts to back them up. Since then, I have learned how far off my opinion was of those leaders.

I also learned lessons about the goals of organizations like the ACLU. The protection of our rights is a strong focus of the ACLU. In my case, haste pushed their good intentions aside and moved the process down one-way roads with no way back to the beginning. As is often the case with one false step, others follow. The lessons I learned about start-overs could also benefit other people and organizations.

I counsel that whatever situation we find ourselves in, we should review all possibilities and not assume that truth is always present. The ACLU did not ask me a single question. I never talked with them. However, they did take action based on what they thought to be the truth. I hold no grudges against them. I forgive them for falling victim to the evil named Haste.

Today, Mr. Rick Danner remains the City of Greer's mayor. He was also a deacon at Victor Baptist Church at the time. The administrator of Greer was also a deacon at another local Church at this time. I loudly pointed out that a deacon should rule for God first and the City of Greer secondly. Years later, I realized that I spoke harshly and wrongly. Today, I better appreciate the horrible situations leaders must navigate through. Good men like them are forbidden from saying the name of Jesus. Gentlemen, let these words be my apology for my remarks. You deserve and now have my most profound appreciation for what you do. Balancing your leadership in a time when sharing the counsel of the Lord Jesus will get you attacked is a horrible place to be for a Christian Leader.

Greer, SC, Mayor Rick Danner

Rules in place in our governments had tied their hands. This tying of their hands was not their fault. As citizens of this great country, we have let loopholes dictate our futures. When we elect or hire Christian leaders, they take on dangerous roles when they do simple things like allowing prayer in public. As a deacon, these restrictions burdened each of these men. I did not appreciate the positions they had to navigate through until later.

Yes, there should be a balance. Our Lord loves Druids, Witches, and Sinners of all types. He will accept them into eternity if they choose Jesus. No matter their past, they can become His children. Our leaders are accountable if they say only the name of Jesus. But they must allow practicers of evil to have events in city parks but not speak of Jesus openly. We are out of balance. Mayor Danner was not worthy of my criticism. Instead, he needed my support and a call to my audiences to support him.

During my last days as an officer, the chief of police (not Chief Crisp or Chief Hamby) was too quick to respond. He made hasty comments to the press that fueled the lies the media promoted about my actions. Those stories were newsworthy, regardless of their truth. That chief mistakenly assumed what he heard to be the whole truth to be just that. Later, he learned the actual truth and supported my internal investigation results. Still, the damage he did seemed too late for him to retract, at least at that time. What was not clear then was that this battle between Good and Evil would take years to finish. Each action from every person during those days turned into the victory I share today. Good won; Evil lost big.

Despite Evil's haste, the Lord Jesus had a plan to use it to His advantage. He has done the same for me many times as well. Everything turned out just as the Lord wanted. Even though I rushed past His hand and whistled for the Lord to catch up, His plan played out. I was wrong with some of my words on television, and I pray those men have forgiven me.

Now let's look at evidence that genuinely emphasizes the character of these men. Mayor Danner has led the City of Greer from a small, unknown town to one recently named one of the best towns in the USA to retire and raise a family. He follows in the footsteps of Mayors Don Wall and Shirley Rollins. These people have contributed to turning Greer into a top place to live. Each of these leaders had to make decisions that supported the voting public. On some occasions, it may have forced them to struggle with the separation of church and government. However, the result emphasizes their victories over Evil that worked to rob Greer of its future. Cities and places have personalities, Evil may have won a few skirmishes in Greer, but Good won the overall battles. The leadership of these mayors championed many of those battles. Thanks to these mayors, Greer is a place of a healthy and happy character. We must also pay tribute to Chief Dean Crisp and Chief Matt Hamby for making the streets of Greer a place of peace and safety.

If you drove through our town twenty years ago and today, you might not recognize the Greer of today. Always be alert when change comes. Please don't rush to push it aside. It just might be the path the Lord wants us to follow. Today, our city is a place where anyone would enjoy living. It is the home of the Greenville Spartanburg International airport, has two interstates nearby, and is centrally located between Greenville, Spartanburg, Asheville, Columbia, Charlotte, and Atlanta. There is much to appreciate in Greer. But one of the most satisfying improvements, for selfish reasons, would be that infamous *Back Row* you read about in many of my stories.

Downtown Greer

I have told many stories that illustrate how we allowed Evil to live alongside us and even fueled the power of Evil with our behaviors in that place. My words can't adequately describe the unhealthy atmosphere in the Back Row. Today, the Back Row is a beautiful city park. I fought, sold drugs, and promoted Evil on the spot where I have since walked with my wife Kim, son Anthony, daughter Melanie, and grandchildren Colin, Jewel, Zoie, and Emma. We have taken treasured pictures and attended concerts and outdoor family movies at Greer City Park. Greer City leadership navigated through times when evil opposed the plans to recapture that land. The Back Row is no more.

Greer City Park (Original Location of the Back Row)

Greer City Park

Other places in Greer once belonged to the evil one. One by one, those places have become places of Peace, where families enjoy themselves. Chief Crisp, the mayors, and the city administrators led this change. Today I know their value, and I respect and applaud them. During my years in law enforcement, I worked to help those who had given up on ever having the hope of obtaining a fresh start. Initially, I thought I would be alone in that desire. However, I honestly say that the city's character that our leaders built also reflects our police officers' character.

In my final days as an officer in Greer, most news media covering me showed no such strength of character. I find that to be true today as well. Today, officers suffer because too many news media members want to major in the seldom. One horrible action does not mean every officer is racist or evil. Some bad officers exist, but the bulk is quality, as my friends at the Greer, South Carolina, Police Department and the Greenville and Spartanburg County Sheriffs departments. Good officers are the majority. Let us all seek the good fruit and not dwell on the few bad apples. All of us, law officers, are embarrassed and saddened by those few officers who harm and kill people. If the news media focused on officers' good, those stories would outweigh the bad by an incredibly colossal margin.

My arrest on the Back Row for distribution of PCP was the first wave of an extended-range plan to make Greer a place where Peace and Hope live. Lots of people played a role in this conversion. The City Council, the Chamber of Commerce, the Fire Department, Leadership Greer, the Commission of Public Works, and many more unnamed people and groups stayed loyal to our city. Together all these people have built a place of integrity. Hope abounds. This city grew over the years while Peace Officers stood guard at the gates. How about some thanks for them in our town and yours?

Where to Get Lessons on Second Chances

I taught a Bible study class intended for struggling people for twelve years. It was in the Mt. Lebanon Baptist Church Ministry Center. This location was across the road from our church and offered those unaccustomed to church a more private experience. There are thousands of such classes all across our world. I was joined in this ministry by other Mt. Lebanon members, Angie Eberly, Ted Hrizak, Dave and Renee Robison, and others who helped me reach those with burdens. We even had breakfast delivered to us by people like the Cantrell family. Our combined efforts saw some who had given up achieve hope for their future and peace for their present. Some of our students are living lives for the Lord today.

We sent invitations to many who came. But some who did not. They would have been embraced as our friends and equals had they come. Second chances began for many during those years. Some became children of a risen king. And yes, we had Witches, Druids, and even Satanists attend. When asked why second chances did not come to others as they did for me, I take this as an opportunity to ask them to review their past crossroads and search for outstretched hands that they pushed away.

My story is not unique. Second chances came to all of us. In that class, we increased awareness that a war exists that aims to stop all of us from realizing the mercy of our Lord Jesus that is always nearby. Another common question was how to get past the quantity and severity of the sins committed. It was a big surprise to most that there was no need to pay for their sins. Learning of His sacrifice on the cross brought many to tears.

Victories came in the battle for the souls of those who had lost hope. I have spoken about places and principalities where angels are assigned. A meeting place like we had, included Guardian Angels who protected the environment against opposing angels of Confusion and Distraction. This "hedge" of protection was vital in our ministry center and church. God's bride, the Church, has such protected places.

I offer this to illustrate that when you are confused about your future, try a local church when you think you have exhausted all resources in your search for help. Their walls are protected against the enemies that work to keep you away from the outstretched arms of our Lord. As a result, you will see more clearly. You will also feel that a second chance is possible. In my case, the second chance was the ten-thousandth chance. The same will be valid for you.

During my struggles on the Back Row, my future wife Kim had a very healthy family and a wonderful church family at Mt. Lebanon Baptist. God was preparing her to become my balance. I would soon meet her. Joy. Hope, Peace, and Beauty accompanied her. A blessing like this awaits all of us.

Fresh-Start Blessings

My efforts to give the hopeless a fresh start cost me my job as a Greer police officer. But that event immediately opened the treasure chest of blessings still appearing today. I paid some dues and stepped into some gopher holes. But, each fall saw me come back stronger. Such is the life of the children of Jesus. Just note that I did not do this climb alone. Jesus is my constant father. He can carry your burdens too.

Today I frequent the very place where evil ruled my life. I can stand in the grass of a city park where the asphalt of the Back Row once was. This little thing gives me great pleasure. It is evidence of an all but impossible miracle. My fresh start took years, but it was worth every step. The same is true for the street in Atlanta, where I bought drugs and lived with the motorcycle gang. Today, that street is a place for families. The lost ground can be re-purposed.

I have learned to pray intercessory prayers for the people in my life, just as my family did for me, I now see what was in their hearts, and I share that same love for the lost and hurting. I pray for protection for my friends and family. I ask that they can see blessings as I have had.

We often take pictures in Greer City Park, where the Back Row was. Beauty pageants, graduations, and holidays are just a few excuses we use to gather for family pictures. I like to sit on one of the swings and pray for strangers walking by. I ask the Lord what to pray for; He occasionally tells me of a specific need. He also makes me aware that some people walking by have no one to pray for them. I choose to fill that role.

When we visited the park today, I never failed to remember how miseries there now are filled with peace. As I glance across the grounds, I see Kim and my family, and my heart leaps in Joy.

Prom photos at Greer City Park

This place of peace was once the home base of many agents of Evil. Today it is the home of Peace, Joy, and Hope. You should see our city and this park if you are in the area, you should visit downtown and this park.

My Unexpected Blessings

Kim and Tony Stewart

Kim (Kimmy) Lemmons Stewart. Like her mother, Jewel is beautiful inside and out. She is the balance I need. I rush, and she steadies me; I push hard, and she pulls gently. I make mistakes; she silently fixes them and smiles through the process. Love came to take up residence in a whole I had in my heart. I had hardened it against more scars. Kim healed those wounds. She used love and patience to do so. She is the love of my life, of which I am so blessed.

Zoie, Anthony, Cara, and Emma Stewart

Our son, Donald Anthony Stewart Jr., will live to a hundred. He is a laid-back, hard-working, amazing dad who can do anything. Anthony is slow to speak, but it is always well thought out. A natural athlete, he excels at anything he touches. His wife, Cara Strait Stewart, likes many of the same things. She is the perfect addition to our family, a fantastic cook, and an excellent mate on more levels than just being his wife. She, too, is steady like Anthony. They parent Zoie Alexis and Emma Faith. These ladies are the joy of our lives. Zoie is tall, kind, and wise beyond her years. Emma is radiant, joyful, witty, and loves to act. I never expected to one day have such amazing people in my family. Today much of what we choose to do is driven by these beautiful girls. I even played with Barbie dolls on occasions-but only when the girls insisted.

Chris, Colin, and Jewel Clare Kittrell

Patrick, Melanie Stewart Henson, Jewel Kittrell

Our daughter, Melanie Heather Stewart Henson, has an energy level beyond measure. She is a natural teacher and an outstanding leader. Like her brother, she is also a competitive athlete and hard worker. Her first husband, Chris Kittell, is still considered family. Their marriage gave Kim and me our first grandchild, Colin Kittrell. Melanie was a great stepmom, and Colin was just two years old when he joined our family. He had a smile that never ended and brought happiness to our households. He grew into a remarkable young man before God called him home at just 21 years of age.

Their daughter Jewel Clare Kittrell is our oldest granddaughter and sets the example for Zoie and Emma to follow. She is driven and a self-starter and over-comer. With talents and beauty seldom equaled, she leaves a blaze in the trail behind her. Today, Melanie's husband, Patrick Henson, is a welcome addition to our family and brings us an intense strength of character. Patrick also has a high energy level and has never met a stranger.

Melanie's daughter, Jewel Clare Kittrell, is our oldest granddaughter and sets the example for Zoie and Emma to follow. She is a self-starter and an overcomer. With talents and beauty seldom equaled, she leaves a blaze in the trail behind her.

These family members are at the top of the blessing list I never expected. Life is a short season. Embrace the people God Sends into your life often. Tell them how wonderful they are.

Today it is easy for me to see why so many second chances came my way. These pictures show family members that I love, but they also offer the leaders of future generations. We all invest parts of ourselves into our family and friends. They, in turn, pass these traits on. It's not just our immediate impact that we should protect. We must also protect future generations.

Strength of Character—
Is it Important?

A nother question I am often asked is why God created us. There are numerous answers that we will only know when we are sitting at the feet of Jesus in eternity. But a good reply is because He wanted our companionship. He gave us free will to become a unique and worthy eternal companion for Him. That free will allows us to create our unique character. No two of us are the same. That makes us unique enough to meet one goal for our creation.

Character is also what attracts us to each other. We choose our friends and our spouse based on their personalities. In my case, I was drawn to Kim, not just because of her beauty but because of her family values. She was generationally blessed, and her strength of character attracted me. She has also instilled this value system in our children and grandchildren.

I learned the hard way that her character has boundaries. Let me explain. Each of us has two boundary lines that, when crossed, drive us into action. One is our love line. When people cross that line, we are pleased and react accordingly. We also have a fear line. When crossed, we respond differently. When my fear line was crossed, I once responded violently. Today, Kim has taught me how to push that fear line farther out—so far out that it is rarely crossed. She also taught me what love means.

If you want to gain favor with someone, spend some time analyzing where these fear lines are. Then work toward pushing past the love line, staying away from the fear line. Simple.

The creator God also has a character. I strongly advise that we all work to avoid crossing the wrong line of the Holy Creator of all that exists. Study his living Word, the Bible. The Old Testament has many examples of his expectations and details things He does not like, some of which bring him to anger. *Exodus 20:1–20, Deuteronomy 18:10, and Leviticus 18:22.* His son Jesus stands ready to intercede for us when we cross the wrong line with his father. The Lord Jesus is our only way to eternity. Even the slightest sins disqualify us from eternal peace in heaven without his forgiveness. What we do not want to do is die and face his judgment with unforgiven sins. Especially like those that anger him. *Romans 13:1–2, Psalm 147:10–11, John 5:30, Ephesians 5:10, Philippians 2:13.* One scripture particularly emphasizes God's desire to protect us—*Proverbs 16.*

As a parent, there comes a time when we must be firm. Our words then change. A study of God's written word emphasizes the strength of his concerns over our sins by the terms he uses.

What Does History Tell Us?

M uch has been done to separate Church from State in our great country. Is this a good thing? We must look to the past for this answer. Here is a good example. The chosen nation of Israel was conquered numerous times before the birth of Christ Jesus. Some of the same factors caused this each time. They made the same mistakes over and over. This series of errors lasted for hundreds of years. Rules of conduct and expectations were in place before they drifted away from the will of the Lord and did not change. Still, they drifted and suffered accordingly. In the separation of church and state question, we have drifted far from what our founding fathers wanted our nation to become.

How did Israel drift? The answer is in the decisions of their leadership. Could we have drifted off course as a country? Israel tended to follow their leaders, some of which were far from spiritually sound. If we only agree with the loudest voice and do not do independent studies on our own, we can expect to one-day fall victim to the same losses the nation of Israel saw. Do the study of our history on your own. Do not make your final decision just on opinions on television or in written media. Instead, look at the Declaration of Independence, the Constitution, and all the supporting information from that time. Read books about our country's fathers. Before starting your study, pray that the Holy Spirit will be your guide, and read the Bible!

You will likely find that we built our great country around early leaders with intentions that differ from the legal experts who interpret our Constitution today. Somehow, we have lost track of their combined character. Our founding fathers welcomed people of all nations and religions. The separation of church and state we battle over today is far from what our forefathers wanted to achieve. They were tired of the Church of England mandating that they had to pay their ministers from their crops even when these crops made no yearly profit. They did not say that Jesus could not be a part of their government. They also did not say that other religions could not have equal representation.

Our nation was built with the character of leaders who did not say to remove Christian prayer from city council meetings. Sadly, much more than prayer in government fell to this attack of Satan. We drifted far from what the founding fathers dreamed that we could be.

How to be Saved?
How to Receive Jesus?

With the sacrifice of Jesus on the cross, we no longer have to pay for our sins. Instead, we only need to ask Jesus to become our Savior, believe He arose from the dead, and ask him to forgive our sins. No sacrificial offering is required, and you can't work your way out of evil. God, the Father, still has expectations, and the rules of behavior created by the eternal God still apply. However, His Son stands in the gap for His children when we cross the wrong line with His Father. In my case, I see many times when God frowned, and Jesus interacted on my behalf, stating that I was one of His children. Jesus loves us so much that the third part of the Holy Trinity, the Holy Spirit, is now among us to give us counsel when we are wise enough to ask.

A word about sin: some sins are addressed by God, using stronger than average words. But any sin disqualifies us from the presence of God. More specifically, what God calls an abomination, Jesus can still forgive. We are all sinners. We all do not qualify to have a seat in heaven at the throne of God. But Jesus changed that with His death and resurrection. Call on Him, accept and believe in Him, and ask for forgiveness. That's the recipe for removing sin. That's the call to action for our descendants. Lastly, don't continue to choose sin over repentance.

Please consider traveling this road to salvation: *Romans 3:23, Romans 3:10-18, Romans 6:23, Romans 5:8, Romans 10:9, Romans 10:13, Romans 5:1, Romans 8:1, Romans 8:39-39*

Road Signs, Crossing Guards, and Intervention

often mention making a list of good and bad things encountered in people's lives. I have found that writing things down forces us to think through events. The result often surprises people. The list should be built around three categories: Road signs, Crossing guards, and intervention from an unseen force like an angel or the Holy Spirit.

- *Road Signs* are people we encounter who stand firm and do not sway in their guidance or influence.
  - o *Road Signs* are easy to spot. A road sign gives us absolute guidance. Stop, go, yield, and other signs are never flexible. They are rigid indicators of a path to follow.
- *Crossing Guards* are often nearby when we make life-altering course changes. These turns may start as minor detours but may evolve into blessed destinations.
  - o *Crossing Guards* are helpful when making course changes in our lives. They can be in the form of people we already know or strangers who appear only once. Crossing guards often coach without even realizing it. Unlike road signs, they often offer gentle advice and can be overlooked accordingly.
- *Intervention* is generally from a heavenly angel. Another kind of intervention can come from the hand of God in the form of His Holy Spirit through visions or signs that could only be from our Lord Jesus.

o *Intervention* is a factor of heavenly actions. And, most often, it is delivered by angels from heaven. Intervention can be sent by our Lord Jesus or given in response to the prayers of our loved ones or church groups who care about us. Intervention is not consistently recognized in real-time. The most potent intervention is when the Holy Spirit guides us through signs, events, or other people. The Holy Spirit frequently speaks His wisdom for us through dreams, visions, and other prominent signs. Intervention can also come through prayers that we make for ourselves or others.

My Crossing Guards

I think it wise that we all know and thank those who guide us wisely. Through words or examples, these people are our heroes. Let us not forget the ancestors before us who prayed for intercession for those descendants they never knew. Let us become Crossing Guards, Life Coaches, and Intercessory prayer warriors for today's and tomorrow's battles.

At this time in my life, burdens still come, but I can navigate them. In November 2021, I lost my twenty-one-year-old grandson Colin Kittrell to a horrible car accident. Two seventeen-year-olds were also lost. Without the peace that comes through my life as a Christian, my family and I would be lost and alone.

I seek an answer to the question of why? I struggle with the silence, and oft-times, no voice is heard. I know that Death is not the name of an angel of my Lord. Instead, Death was dispatched by the enemy of life himself, Satan. Yes, he had to have the permission of the Creator God. And, I know that Colin's death had a purpose that is yet unknown to us. Many life coaches have appeared to all of us. Comfort has come. So, onward I go. However, I have a new passion. I see a vision for book 3. Writing is what I am to do but only as a hope seller. So, book three must continue this goal.

However, my life stories have been told from my perspective so far. Next, I will write from the viewpoints of the angels standing in the gap for me (and all of us) and from the fallen angels' perspectives. I will use my life battles to illustrate the conversations and strategic plans that must have happened. My next book will focus on actual events in my life from an angelic viewpoint. It will be a fantastical version of a true story.

This chapter closes the book by listing a few wise people the Lord Jesus sent into my life and family. When making lists, you may want to include one like this one. The chances are that some of your crossing guards were never noticed or thanked. Also, take a quiet and prayerful walk through your town. Pray for the clearness of thoughts. You will hear the silent voices of many new allies of hope as I do on the streets of Greer, South Carolina, Greenville, and Spartanburg counties, and in the Blue Ridge region and community where I live.

This list is not inclusive. Many other coaches appeared at my life's crossroads. *Some I will only know of when I met them on the streets of Glory.*

Many thanks to my Life Coaches:

Attorneys: Jack Lynn and Matt Henderson

Judges: Midred Stokes, Hank Mims, Carey Werner

Public Officials: Mayor Rick Danner, Councilman Mike Barnes, Joseph Farley

Police officers: Chief Dean Crisp, Chief Matt Hamby, Sheriff Hobart Lewis, Sheriff Chuck Wright, Officer Travis Stamey, Detective Gary Gilstrap, and Sergeant Jimmy Guthrie.

Trusted friends and business associates: Ted Hrizak, Bruce Redmon, Jack Dix, Stuart Brinsfield, Oliver Whitaker, Scott Crider, Haven Owens, Wade Moose, Trudy Phillips, Kirk Phillips, David Steele. Steve Smith, Ron Norman, Kyle Herman.

Men and Women of God: Pastor and Police Chapman Keith Kelly, Police Chaplain Benny Babb, Roger Henson, Pastor Doug Brown, Kenneth Southerlin, Bud Turner, Quain Suddeth, Alvin Baker, Michael Campbell, Michael and Maudine Cantrell, Michael Aaron Cantrell, Marshall Allen, David Welchel, Charles and Bertha Fisher, Bill and Judy Bright, Elliott and Shirl Wooten, Angie Eberly, Dave, and Renee Robison.

The Senior Citizens at Mt Lebanon Baptist Church, Pastor Eddie Connors and Members at Apalache Baptist, Pastor Drew Hines, and Members at Washington Baptist.

Athletes, I enjoyed calling teammates: Anthony Stewart, Melanie Stewart, Dennis Gibson, Bennie Sloan, Johnny Owens, David Mason, Sammy Campbell, Doug Brown, Kyle Herman, Michael Campbell, Ronnie Nobles, Fred Battenfield, and many others.

Other Heroes I admire:

Country Music Star Aaron Tippin. Aaron grew up with my wife, Kim. We are blessed to know him, his wife Thea, his sons, Tom and Teddy, and daughter Charla, a long-time friend of my daughter, Melanie. Aaron has a strength of character equaled by few. He is a patriot and a Christian, and his music proves that fact. He is also a hero of the Toys for Tots campaigns.

Aaron Tippin, Renee and Dave Robison, Kim and Tony Stewart

OJ and Chandra Brigance. OJ was a Baltimore Raven Football player. Today he has ALS but continues to inspire others. I was honored to meet OJ and Chandra while providing counsel on his Smart House System.

Rick and Christine Kovach and family. I met this family as a consultant on their Smart House system. This family proves that you can still honor the Lord Jesus once success comes your way.

May God bless you, my readers. Know this: wonderful gifts are planned for us throughout this earthly visit. But the eternal reward cannot be imagined. I hope to see you there.

There is always hope for the hopeless.
Second chances and fresh starts are abundant.

CPSIA information can be obtained
at www.ICGtesting.com
Printed in the USA
LVHW081346110822
725656LV00010B/167